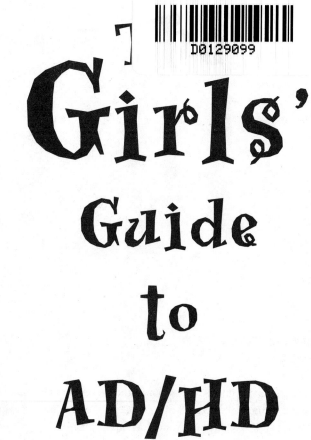

The Girls' Guide to AD/HD

Don't Lose This Book!

Beth Walker

Woodbine House ▪ 2004

All rights reserved under International and Pan-American Copyright Conventions.
Published in the United States of America by Woodbine House, Inc., 6510 Bells Mill Rd., Bethesda, MD 20817. 800-843-7323. www.woodbinehouse.com

Library of Congress Cataloging-in-Publication Data

Walker, Beth, date.
  The girls' guide to ADHD : don't lose this book! / Beth Walker.— 1st ed.
     p. cm.
  Includes index.
  ISBN 1-890627-56-9
  1. Attention-deficit-disordered children—Juvenile literature. 2. Teenage girls—Mental health—Juvenile literature. I. Title.
  RJ506.H9W347 2004
  618.92'8589—dc22

                                                                    2004020966

Manufactured in the United States of America

10 9 8 7 6 5 4 3 2 1

To my family, with love.

Table
of
Contents

Foreword

Congratulations! You are reading this fabulous book about girls with AD/HD. And you haven't even lost the book yet.

By reading even this far, you've begun finding out about AD/HD (Attention-Deficit/Hyperactivity Disorder), and also understanding thousands of girls who cope with AD/HD every day. People with AD/HD often have loads of ideas, think and put things together in unusual ways, and are energetic, funny, sometimes brilliant or creative, and always unpredictable.

Typically, the problems people with AD/HD face get a lot more attention than the good stuff about having AD/HD does. Also, boys with AD/HD have gotten more attention over the years. So girls, it's your turn!

You need your own book on AD/HD because girls are different from boys (you knew that), but you might not realize that girls have some different AD/HD symptoms and problems than boys. For example, girls are more likely to be depressed or dreamy; boys are more likely to be loud or rowdy. As you might expect, the loud or rowdy boys usually get attention; the dreamy or depressed girls often don't.

This book presents information using three different characters, each a composite—a mix—of traits that can belong to girls with AD/HD. The person in this book who does most of the "talking" is Maddy. She is chatty and funny, but she also has to deal with depression. Helen has a hard time paying attention and keeping track of things (you never knew anybody like that). She also likes science and riding her bike. And Bo, pronounced BOH, a nickname (more about that later), worries a lot, tends to daydream, and likes dogs. Even though the girls presented in this book are fictional, they are based on very bright, very engaging, and very real girls with AD/HD, only all mixed up into three separate girls, speaking throughout this book.

And another thing. Girls in middle school and high school can be called girls, teenagers, young adults, and young women. Who are you, anyway? Since you can't answer back, this book refers to you all, collectively, as girls.

One last thing. This book promises that it is NOT yet-another-compendium-of-suggestions you've already heard a thousand times. Any mention of Using Your Planner and Making Lists will be preceded by some kind of warning sign or apology.

On the other hand, the obvious tips are included because, what the heck, maybe you're lucky and this is your introduction to AD/HD. For you, the obvious won't be obvious until after you've read the book.

Even though life as a girl with AD/HD isn't always easy, you probably find ways to keep life lively. Read on to learn about good stuff, normal stuff, brain stuff, and, well, stuff that isn't in any other book for girls with AD/HD.

Chapter 1

AD/HD:

What Does It Mean, Anyway?

AD/HD means Attention-Deficit/Hyperactivity Disorder, and sometimes it's called ADD, which means you subtract the word Hyperactivity.

Subtract sounds like math, doesn't it? Math is not one of my favorite subjects, except that I do have a really good teacher. His name is Mr. Brown, and although it sounds like a made-up name, it isn't.

No. Wait. I was trying to tell you about AD/HD. Well, actually, I've already summed up AD/HD pretty well. (Summed up AD/HD—get it? Joke about math?)

People with AD/HD don't focus, or pay attention, the way other people do. They have a deficit of attention, which means not enough attention, which is why teachers sometimes tell me to pay attention.

It's not that I don't pay attention. I pay attention. It just isn't always what I'm supposed to be paying attention to.

That reminds me. I haven't introduced myself. My name is Maddy. Short for Madeleine.

This is mostly my book, but sometimes, my friends Bo and Helen are in it too. (It has like 17 research papers worth of stuff in it, too.) Usually, if you see the word "I" in this book, I'm the one doing the talking. You'll be able to tell who's talking because you'll see that person's name in front of her comments.

AD = What Focus?

The AD—attention-deficit part—means that I get distracted.[1] Other kids some-how mostly concentrate on what the teacher is talking about when she goes on and on about the quadratic equation or the history of Estonia, and they remember what time their mom told them to be home after school.

Not me. I mostly cannot concentrate, no matter how hard I try.

I start off paying attention. Really, I try hard to stay tuned in. But a lot of the time, something else steals my attention. Say, I get hot, so I look out the window at the sun. Then I think about how the builders put in the windows, then whether I could build a house, and pretty soon, it's ten minutes later, the teacher is asking me a question, and it isn't about architecture. When the teacher calls on me, I'm embar-rassed. So sometimes I get mad and smart off, then get in big trouble for my big mouth. Then I have to try not to cry.

Everybody gets distracted like this some of the time. People with AD/HD get distracted like this a lot of the time.

Most people with AD/HD also have the opposite problem sometimes—it's called hyperfocus, which means to concentrate on something intensely. In art class, I get so involved that I lose track of time. That's the good news. But sometimes I don't hear something the teacher says because I am so lost in the project. That's the bad news.

So the good news is that you can concentrate on things that you find interesting. And the bad news is that you don't get to pick what you hyperfocus on.

Even the good news can be bad news. Some people look at that kind of super-concentration, then say, "See? You concentrate on things when you want to. Most of the time you just don't try."

Well, I do try, and it doesn't work. Maybe you know this feeling.

It all comes back to AD/HD, and how it affects the way your brain works.

H = Maybe Hyperactivity

So far we've covered the AD parts of AD/HD. Time to talk about the H. (Sounds like we're brought to you by the letters H and D, and the numbers....) H stands for Hyperactivity. Technically, hyperactivity means excessive activity. Well, let me tell you, I'm a slug. I am definitely not hyperactive.[2]

In elementary school, hyperactive boys are pretty obvious. They spin around, jumping and talking loudly as though they've just eaten an entire pound of refined sugar. Those boys.

But girl-hyperactivity doesn't always look like boy-hyperactivity. Hyperactive girls, even really athletic girls, are often not as rowdy as the little hyper boys. Instead of

---

[1] You might think AD means the year, like Anno Domini, year of Our Lord, the calendar, right? Well, it does. But in this case it also stands for attention deficit.

[2] The opposite of hyperactive is hypoactive (slug).

Helen: My name is Helen, and I definitely have the bouncy, let's-get-going approach. My idea of fidgeting is jumping on the trampoline. In fact, I think my parents got the trampoline just to give my younger brother (the one with AD/HD) and me someplace safe to jump.

Bo: Hi. I'm Bo.[3] I am *not* hyperactive. I can sit very still. Outside, birds come right up to me.

Maddy: Bo and Helen, it's not quite your turn. Yes, I know waiting is hard... for girls with AD/HD, especially!

bouncing around the classroom, they doodle, draw, whisper to their neighbors, fidget in their seat (maybe practicing for a part in Cirque de Soleil or gymnastics, bending and twisting), but not quite as obvious as some of the very active (not to say frenetic) boys. And that's part of the reason why most of the AD/HD research is about younger boys.

Now that I think about it, maybe I am hyperactive. It is nearly impossible for me to sit still.[4] And my notebook is more of an anime (pronounced ah nih may, that Japanese sort of comic book?) and less of a notebook with notes.

D = Disorder

D is for Disorder.

When you talk about AD/HD, the word disorder means a condition that falls outside the realm of "normal" (whatever that is). Lots of kids talk extra, get distracted, and lose things. This set of behaviors is normal in small batches. For kids with AD/HD, this set of behavior is "normal" in large batches. The large batches factor—that's what turns the whole thing into a disorder.

I also think it's funny that this condition or syndrome uses the word disorder. That's my favorite word out of Attention Deficit/Hyperactivity Disorder. Disorder: That's my life. I don't understand how everybody else can remember to hand in homework and write down assignments and all that. For most people, this seems to come naturally, or at least way more easily than it does for me.

FACTOID: How Common Is AD/HD?
Between 6 and 9 percent of the population in the U.S. is affected, which translates into millions of people with AD/HD.

---

[3] Bo: My name isn't really Bo. It's Ethelwyn. But when I was one year old and just starting to talk, the closest I could get to pronouncing Ethelwyn was "Bo." It stuck. And it's way easier to live with than Ethelwyn.

[4] Sitting still: that's a hard one. My aunt is a Quaker, and got married at a Quaker meeting. Do you know what Quaker meetings are like? Everybody is sitting in a pew or on a chair and is completely still and silent. Once in a while, somebody says something. My aunt's wedding took forever. It was torture.

Girls vs. Boys

Girls don't get identified as having AD/HD nearly as often as boys, and usually girls are diagnosed when they are closer to our age, in middle school or junior high school or even high school (or college!). Why? I know I said this before. But here it is again. Because often girls aren't so obviously hyperactive as those elementary school boys. My mom says I was a daydreamy kid, plenty bright, and easy to ignore. Lots of little girls with AD/HD are like that. Imagine which one gets the attention: the daydreaming girl, or the extremely busy boy?

Also, this makes me wonder if the daydreamy boys get ignored, too? My bet is that those boys get overlooked, too.

One bad thing about being a girl with AD/HD is that we seem to be more likely to blame ourselves if we don't get homework done or leave a room in a mess. "Why can't I do it, when everybody else can?" is more likely to serve as a refrain-for-life for girls than boys.

Anyway, a diagnosis of AD/HD helps girls understand why other kids get homework assignments done and rooms picked up. You have more energy to deal with the problem once you stop wasting energy on feeling bad about yourself. I don't know why we girls are more likely to feel bad about ourselves, but studies show it's true. Let's blame estrogen—but I'll get to that in Chapter 4.

FACTOID: AD/HD in Boys and in Girls

Check this out. Boys really do show hyperactivity differently from girls (yeah, yeah, not all boys and girls—if you have "boy" symptoms, you're lucky, because you probably found out about the AD/HD sooner).

Boys	Girls
Run around the classroom	Fidget in your seat
Burst out talking	Whisper to your neighbor
Climb the walls	Climb your seat

Researchers estimate that AD/HD is way under-diagnosed in girls. Some estimate that as many as 75 percent of girls with AD/HD aren't diagnosed! This translates into 3 or 4 boys diagnosed for every girl diagnosed.

AD/HD Characteristics

Doctors and psychologists who are trained in this business work with you to find out whether you have AD/HD. The treatment chapters describe a little bit about the process of getting diagnosed, but not a whole lot, since new tests and procedures come out pretty often.

The Upside of Having AD/HD

If you have AD/HD, some of these might describe you. You might have:
◎ A kind of interpersonal charm or "something extra."
◎ A lively sense of humor or play.
◎ An ability to engage fully; to focus intensely on anything of interest.
◎ An empathetic and compassionate nature. You are able to put yourself in another's place and imagine what the person is feeling.
◎ An ability to quickly forgive—maybe that's the upside of forgetfulness!
◎ A lot of ideas.
◎ An ability to connect facts and observations in original ways, and connect ideas that others might not.
◎ A lot to contribute, partly because you think in unusual patterns.
◎ A closeness to and a love for the natural world, including pets and wild animals.
◎ A lot of energy.
◎ A good time when a lot of things are going on at the same time.
◎ An ability to do a lot of things at the same time.
◎ A passion for something.
◎ An adventurous nature.
◎ A strong will, an in-built determination.
In short, you are truly an original!

The Downside of Having AD/HD

You might have trouble:
◎ Paying attention and following instructions.
◎ Sitting still.
◎ Getting started and figuring out what to do first.
◎ Finishing homework or other tasks.
◎ Switching to new tasks.
◎ Getting distracted when too much else is going on.
◎ Remembering things, such as what the assignments are, and to turn your assignments in, if you do the homework.
◎ Dealing with your emotions, because you have a lot of them (including frustration).
◎ Fitting in with other people your age.
◎ Getting rid of unpleasant emotions or thoughts.
◎ Falling asleep and waking up.
◎ Thinking before you speak or act. You say things or do things when they occur to you, rather than thinking through possible results (that is, what will happen if you say or do the thing).
◎ Extreme sensitivity to your surroundings—clothing tags bother you. This is called tactile defensiveness.

AD/HD QUIZ: Do you or don't you?

The statement:	Doesn't describe me at all.	Describes me a little.	Describes me a lot of the tme.	That's me exactly!
People think I am funny, or that I have a lively sense of humor.				
I have a hard time paying attention for a long time. Lectures are really hard.				
I can really concentrate on things that I find interesting.				
I fidget, rather than sit still.				
I can feel your pain. No, really, I can imagine what it feels like to be another person. Sometimes it's a character in a book or a movie, other times it's somebody in my school.				
I have a hard time starting a big project. I don't know what to do first.				
It's hard to finish assignments.				
I have a hard time remembering homework assignments.				
It's hard to fall asleep.				
I have a lot of ideas, and I'm always finding new ways to do things.				
I have a lot of energy.				
I can do a lot of things at the same time.				
TOTALS. **Yes, more math.** **Add them up:**				

An AD/HD Quiz

This quiz at left lists characteristics that are used to describe people with AD/HD. So fill this out—check one answer for each item listed. (Filling out the quiz won't give you a real diagnosis, but it's interesting, anyway.)

Remember, even if some of these feel like you are being vain, tell the truth anyway. You can always erase it later, so nobody knows.

Scoring Your Quiz

By the way, any quiz you take that is in THIS BOOK? You get a perfect score.

Now, count up the totals. I know, this is a little like fortune cookies or horoscopes, because everyone does some of these things some of the time. Still, tally that total. What number did you get?

- ◎ **That's Me Exactly** column: Score 6 plus, you probably have AD/HD.
- ◎ **Describes Me A Lot of the Time** column: Score 9 plus, you probably have AD/HD.
- ◎ Sum of the **Exactly** and **A Lot** columns: Score of 8 or more, you may very well have AD/HD.
- ◎ Sum of the **Doesn't Describe Me at All** or **Describes Me a Little** columns: 10 or more, you probably don't have AD/HD.
- ◎ Every other scoring combination: You may, just maybe, have AD/HD.

What to do with these scores: If your totals are pretty high on the Exactly or A Lot columns, or if you think you might have AD/HD and nobody has ever diagnosed it, you might want to tell a parent or an adult you trust, or your family doctor.

Which Parts Do You Have?

You can have AD/HD even if you mostly have the AD or mostly the H. This is true for both boys and girls. According to experts, there are three basic types of AD/HD:

AD/HD Types: Attention Deficit/Hyperactivity Disorder
- ◎ **AD/HD-I**—AD/HD primarily inattentive, no hyperactivity (mostly day-dreamy, not so spontaneous)
- ◎ **AD/HD-HI**—AD/HD primarily hyperactive-impulsive (mostly spontaneous)
- ◎ **AD/HD-C**—AD/HD combined inattention and hyperactivity (day-dreamy AND spontaneous)

This book isn't going to use the dash-letter thingies. I included this information just so you can see how adults might think about it.

QUIZ on Day-Dreaminess
(how you rate on AD/HD inattentive symptoms)

Mark the rows that describe you (or whoever it is you know who has or might have AD/HD):

Maddy's Description	Boring Description	If it fits. check it.
1. I sometimes don't know I didn't hear the teacher until it's time to turn in assignments I never knew were due. Sometimes teachers tell me I'm not listening, but I'm not doing it on purpose, honest. I just can't help it.	1. Doesn't pay attention. Scattered.	
2. I don't read the assignment or test question correctly, so that the answer I put down is the answer to what I thought it said, instead of the answer to the actual question.	2. Misreads test and homework questions.	
3. In math, I work too fast and skip steps in figuring out the answer. In writing, I forget to write words. Even though I know what I'm trying to say or do, I get it wrong, wrong, wrong.	3. Doesn't work carefully or check work.	
4. The one copy I have of the homework that the teacher just gave me gets lost between the time I get it and the time I get to my locker.	4. Loses stuff. Disorganized.	
5. I never know what time it is and I don't wear a watch because I have lost too many of them.	5. Doesn't keep track of time.	
Write your total score. Mine is 5	**TOTAL YOU CHECKED (between 0 and 5):**	

Scoring Your Quizzes

◎ **Day Dreaminess**: Score 0-2 is standard day-dreaminess. Score 3-5, you are an official day-dreamer.

◎ **Spontaneity**: Score 0-1 is standard action. Score 2-5, your action moves into hyper-action.

◎ If you score high on both quizzes, you might have the combined type of AD/HD. That's the most common type diagnosed in girls, by the way.

What to do with these scores: Mostly, these are for fun. But if you score high on any of these, or think you might have AD/HD and nobody has ever diagnosed

QUIZ on Spontaneity
(how you rate on AD/HD hyperactive/impulse symptoms)

Mark the rows that describe you (or whoever it is you know who has or might have AD/HD):

Maddy's Description	Boring Description	If it fits, check it.
1. Sitting still isn't only hard, it's nearly impossible. I like to sit on my chair with my legs crossed, or maybe with one knee up, or one leg over my neck.	1. Fidgets.	
2. I get in trouble because I talk too much and I know I shouldn't interrupt but what if I think of something that's funny or soooo correct? And if it's especially important, I need to say it right away, because otherwise I'll forget it.	2. Talkative.	
3. I seem to make a lot of noise even when I'm drawing.	3. Noisy.	
4. On good days, you can almost read what I write.	4. Bad handwriting.	
5. Waiting for anything=poison. Waiting is FRUSTRATING!	5. Hates to wait.	
Write your total score. Mine is 4	**TOTAL YOU CHECKED (between 0 and 5):**	

it, you might want to tell a parent or an adult you trust, or your family doctor. This is repeated from the last quiz, yeah, but only because what if you skipped a quiz that came before this one?

One Way to Think about AD/HD

One thing that helped me deal with the fact that I have AD/HD was knowing that I only have it because of the way my brain is wired[5], not because I'm a bad kid. I'm really not lazy and stupid. It's that my brain is built differently from the brains of most people in the world. It *feels* like it's my fault that I forget my homework, or lose it, or don't hand it in, or forget to brush my teeth. But it isn't exactly my fault. It's that I concentrate differently from the way most people do. Another way to put it is that my memory works, but not like it does for most people.

---

[5] That is WIRED not WEIRD. I love anagrams....

AD/HD is a syndrome. Syndrome means "a group of symptoms that occur together." That means that people with AD/HD share some symptoms in common—not all, but some. Even so, they all have AD/HD.

One example of a disease that has a lot of different symptoms is pneumonia, which is a lung infection. Each of the following combinations of symptoms can mean you have pneumonia:

- ◎ A dry cough and tiredness, followed occasionally by a rash and phlegm (which is pronounced "flem," and is a polite word for mucus or snot).
- ◎ Cough, fever, and pain on the side of the affected lung. Streaks of blood may be seen in the phlegm. (I'm using phlegm, because everyone needs more words that start with ph.)
- ◎ The infection begins with aches and pains, fever, and headache, followed by a cough that eventually produces phlegm.

Let's see. That means you can have pneumonia with or without a rash, with or without aches, with or without headache. About the only thing common to all three of these sets of symptoms: phlegm.

In other words, one person can have pneumonia with one set of symptoms, and another person can have it with a mostly different set of symptoms, but both people have the same thing: pneumonia. In the same way, people with AD/HD can have some symptoms in common, but not all.

And another thing. . .

If you've ever heard people say that AD/HD "isn't real," those people probably want everything to be ON or OFF—clear cut. I figure these people are (choose all that apply):

A. inflexible

B. unaware that they know or work with people who have AD/HD.

It can be hard to pick us out because lots of us with AD/HD are smart, even really smart, and creative. So we learn how to get by and fit in. We often blend in rather than stand out, especially as we get older.

AD/HD Rules To Live By

Actually, having rules for AD/HD is pretty funny, if you think about it, because people with AD/HD forget rules.

Rule 1: Never, ever think that AD/HD is your fault. It isn't. It is not a character flaw. You aren't bad. It's your biology and neurochemistry, not your fault. (For more about this, see Chapters 2 and 3.)

Rule 2: Remember that even though AD/HD is not your fault, it *is* your responsibility. You get the good stuff[6] and the bad stuff that goes with it.

Rule 3: If you aren't getting the support you need, find it. Support means finding someone on your side. In the best of circumstances, you can count on some people,

---

[6] Yes. There is good stuff. It's in a chapter cleverly titled "The Good Stuff."

AD/HD Myth and Reality

Myth. AD/HD isn't real. It's a government plot to drug the children and not let them be free. Haven't you seen reports in the media that we're overdosing our children?

Reality. Haven't you done any research on the subject? Dr. Joseph Biederman, a physician and researcher at Harvard, has declared that AD/HD is the most studied and most understood disorder in the entire field of psychiatry/psychology. Further, brain scans have proven inherent brain differences between the brains of people with AD/HD vs. those without AD/HD. Further, the neurotransmitter action as it relates to AD/HD has been studied a lot. (Neurotransmitters are talked about in Chapter 3.)

Myth. AD/HD? Oh, my brother had that, and he outgrew it.

Reality. No, he just learned to cope with it. AD/HD is a neurological condition, the way you are wired. That's not something you outgrow. True, when people with AD/HD get older, we sometimes seem to be more focused. That's because, when we are older, we can do more things that interest us, so of course we are more focused. We still have AD/HD. We aren't stuck in school studying things we aren't interested in, which makes AD/HD obvious.

maybe your parents, coaches, teachers, a psychologist or school counselor, an aunt or uncle, or a priest or minister or rabbi or whatever you have if you practice an organized religion. You get the idea. You have to have support, even if you have to give it to yourself by reading books like this. And for more things you can do, check out the treatment chapters.

Three rules are enough. Phew!

A Brief History of AD/HD

First, I was born. At that point, it was too late. I had AD/HD. Wait. This is a history of AD/HD, not my history.

1902: A physician in Britain, Dr. George Still[7] described a condition of a bunch of kids who lacked "inhibitory volition" (that is, they were impulsive) and were "passionate and defiant." He said that this was a brain problem, and not because the kids had bad parents. This was a shocking statement back then. He called the condition "Defect of Moral Control."

---

[7] His name really was Dr. George Still, and his patients really couldn't sit still. This joke is not a joke.

1917-18: A viral encephalitis epidemic (that is, an epidemic of brain infection caused by a virus) caused a lot of people's behavior to change. They began to act a lot like people who have what is now called AD/HD. This supported the idea that AD/HD behavior is linked to the brain. This was called "Post-Encephalitic Behavior Disorder."

1930: The syndrome was renamed "Organic Drivenness."

1937: Dr. Charles Bradley, a pediatrician at the Emma Bradley Hospital in Rhode Island, gave some kids with what is now called AD/HD an amphetamine—Benzedrine™ tablets, to be specific.[8] It reduced the symptoms of AD/HD, and is the predecessor of Ritalin® and related stimulant medicines available today. The kids called these pills "arithmetic pills," because with the medicine they could sit still and do their math homework, times tables, addition, subtraction.

1940-50s: The syndrome was renamed "Minimal Brain Dysfunction" partly because, during World War II, doctors treated lots of soldiers who had head injuries, and some of them displayed shorter attention spans and hyperactivity as a result of the injuries.

1956: Doctors began prescribing Ritalin® (methylphenidate) for AD/HD.

1980: *The Diagnostic and Statistical Manual*, third edition, by the American Psychiatric Association, also known as DSM-III, defined the syndrome as "Attention-Deficit Disorder— ADD—with or without Hyperactivity."

1994: *The Diagnostic and Statistical Manual*, fourth edition, by the American Psychiatric Association, a.k.a. DSM-IV, defined the syndrome as Attention-Deficit/Hyperactivity Disorder. This led to the current abbreviation: AD/HD.

---

[8] For more more about medicine that can help AD/HD, check out the treatment chapters.

The Back Page
• • •

Cheat Sheet

AD/HD stands for Attention-Deficit/Hyperactivity Disorder, which is one way of describing how some brains work. People with AD/HD are often high-energy, good at doing a lot of things at once, funny or compassionate, and capable of putting ideas together in unusual ways, along with being forgetful, prone to losing things, and impulsive and easily distracted.

Millions of people have AD/HD. Girls are diagnosed less often than boys are, though. If you think you have AD/HD but you've never been diagnosed, talk about it with an adult you trust. And keep reading to learn more.

• • •

Ask Ms. ADDvice Lady

Dear Ms. ADDvice Lady:

I hate having something that makes me feel different. I tried ignoring it, but the AD/HD doesn't leave me alone. Do you have any suggestions about how to stop hating having AD/HD?

Hates Hating AD/HD

Dear Hates Hating:

This is hard. It took me a long time to accept the fact that I have AD/HD and always will have it. Like you, I wanted to be "like everyone else." The problem is that no one is like everyone else. So, trying to pick who you would like to be like is a silly way to spend your time.

Remember to tell yourself the good things about AD/HD, and let the bad feelings wash over you until you can let them go. You are going to feel the way you feel, but you can train yourself out of having your upset over having AD/HD run your life. After all, what choice do you have about having AD/HD? None. So learning to accept what is can help you live more fully.

This is probably a totally unsatisfactory answer. But it is true. Every time you hate AD/HD, remind yourself of the good things about it. Remind yourself that when you grow up, you can pick something to do that interests you so the AD/HD won't be so awful on a daily basis, anyway.

Then try to forgive yourself for having faults.

And use the energy that you could spend hating AD/HD on things that help you deal with AD/HD symptoms, which will make you feel better about yourself and the AD/HD.

Then keep going.

Ms. ADDvice Lady

...

Fun Facts to Forget

Dr. Heinrich Hoffman wrote books on medicine and psychiatry, and other things, too, including a book of poetry for his three-year-old son about lots of kinds of children. One of the children he wrote about was a fictitious boy in a story named "The Story of Fidgety Philip." Fidgety Philip likely had AD/HD, which is kind of a "so what," except that the story was written before anyone had figured out there was such a thing as AD/HD—in 1854.

...

Chapter 2

Geography of the Wired Brain

So, my brain is different.

How obvious can you get—everybody's brain is different, you're thinking.

Well, yes. But AD/HD brains have consistent differences.[1] The differences aren't that big a deal: you are mostly just like everybody else. But the differences help explain the AD/HD parts of you.

Brains: The Difference

AD/HD brains are a little bit different from non-AD/HD brains. Part of what's different is the size of different parts of the brains. Part of what's different is the neurochemistry (the molecules your brain uses). And all of this is made even more interesting by adolescence—just in case puberty wasn't fun enough, on its own, without AD/HD.

AD/HD brains are slightly different between genders. This helps explain some of the differences between boys and girls with AD/HD.

---

[1] Consistent differences? Pretty good joke. Especially since consistency means repeatedly doing the same thing, which to people with AD/HD is boring and frustrating.

Brain Structures

Scientists use different machines, such as MRIs, to take pictures of your brain in cross-section. These pictures have been used to figure out how brains work, including how AD/HD brains work.

MRI

MRI, which stands for magnetic resonance imaging, works kind of like sonar. In sonar, sound waves are sent out. When they bounce off something, a computer records and analyzes the returning sound. This analysis reveals the shape of the object. Submarines use sonar. Bats do too.

MRI works like bat echoes, except instead of sending out sound waves, it uses radio waves (but not ones you can hear on the radio in the car).

Helen: Bats are so cool. Have you ever seen any flying at night? I have even seen some in the middle of the day. Once, my bike club went riding, and right on this big rock on a hillside were a whole bunch of small bats hanging upside down, in broad daylight. I woke one up while it was trying to sleep, I think.
Sleep. Falling asleep. That's hard sometimes for people with AD/HD, too. Sleep? No, we were talking about sleeping bats. Bats. Sonar. Oh, yeah...MRI!

Anyway, if you get an MRI done, you mostly lie very still for maybe an hour, inside the MRI machine. To make sure you are still, you are only allowed to sleep four hours the night before you get an MRI, so that you are relaxed and sleepy. That way, it's easy for your brain to shift into a drowsy state, where not much is happening, at least on a conscious level. You're too tired to even be nervous. Not that lying still is anything to be nervous about.

MRI uses a great big magnet. You get on a table that slides into a big tube, called a bore (which it is really—boring to have an MRI done, that is). A big thrumming sound grumbles loudly all around you as the MRI cranks up energy to create an enormous magnet. You have to take off jewelry and anything metal before you even walk into the room with the bore, because otherwise the magnet is so strong that metal objects fly across the room to it and you can get hurt if they hit you. (But it doesn't suck the fillings out of your teeth. That would be gross.)

Anyway, you get on a table that slides until the part of you being tested is in this machine. The magnet is so strong that it puts energy into the molecules in your head. The machine then breaks the magnetic field (turns off the magnet) so the extra energy bounces out again. But the trick is that each kind of tissue releases the energy a little differently. That difference is recorded, then that data is used to create a detailed picture of your brain at that specific location, or plane. Next, the table you are on moves into the machine a tiny bit further. This repeats, over and over. Each set of data creates a kind of snapshot, and you move a little bit at a time to get a lot of cross sections of your brain. Cross sections are described in the next section.

The energy that is released is picked up as, I am not making this up, radio waves. Very sensitive receivers pick up these signals. The results end up looking like a lot of X-rays, except that the images are taken using radio waves, not X-rays.

MRI picks up enough data to show both the shape of the object (like sonar), and what kind of tissue it is taking a picture of (which sonar can't).

To get an idea of how this works, start with an apple.

Cut side to side

Cut side to side (an apple cut side-to-side, not a brain), it looks like this.

cut top to bottom

If you use another apple and cut it top to bottom, the slice looks like this.

So, MRI can take images of a slice of the brain, either top to bottom or side to side, except of a brain, not an apple. This slice is referred to as a cross section. MRIs take a whole bunch of cross sections.

fMRI

fMRI is another kind of MRI, where the *f* stands for functional. In fMRI, the machine first takes a normal, high-resolution (very detailed) MRI image. In fMRI, a second step follows. In the case of AD/HD brain research, for example, a researcher then asks the person in the MRI to perform a task such as trying to recall a list of words that someone read to her earlier. While she is trying to recall the words, the MRI takes a lot of pictures, but these are low-resolution, which means the images are fuzzier.

Now, why take pictures first when you are relaxed, then when you are thinking hard about a certain thing?

Because, when any part of your body is working hard, it needs more blood, more energy. Same goes for your brain. The fMRI images show the parts of the brain getting more energy.

So the machine takes lots of pictures every second. By taking pictures of a brain that is concentrating on something, the pictures show which parts of the brain are getting used.

MRI shows a kind of snapshot, while the fMRI pictures are more like a movie, or at least like a flip book, showing what the brain looks like over time while it is busy.

PET Scans

Scientists also use other kinds of imaging, such as PET scanning, which is positron emission tomography (tah MOG grah fee). PET scanning is done only in research institutes, because to use it, the researchers need to inject you with radioactive material. (Not enough to make you grow a second head or anything. Just a tiny bit.) The machines can track the radioactivity.

Helen: Kind of glow-in-the-dark molecules. After all, it's dark inside your head.

Using Brain Images

At first, researchers used these images to help them figure out what parts of the brain were used when. So, for example, researchers asked a volunteer to do something like read a list. Then the volunteer tried to recall what was on the list. The researchers took brain pictures, using PET scans or fMRI, while the volunteer was doing the task. The resulting images showed which parts of the brain were getting used, because that part would get more blood pumping to it.

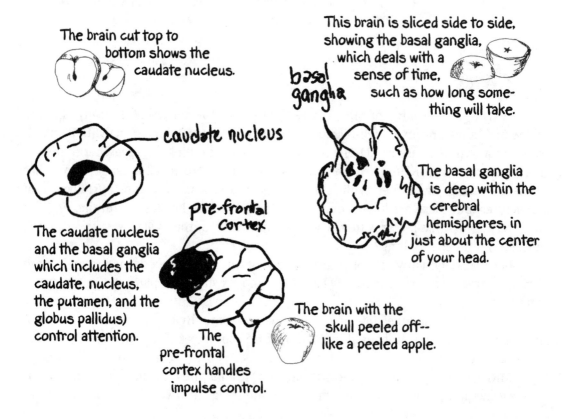

The brain cut top to bottom shows the caudate nucleus.

This brain is sliced side to side, showing the basal ganglia, which deals with a sense of time, such as how long something will take.

basal ganglia

caudate nucleus

The caudate nucleus and the basal ganglia which includes the caudate, nucleus, the putamen, and the globus pallidus) control attention.

pre-frontal cortex

The pre-frontal cortex handles impulse control.

The basal ganglia is deep within the cerebral hemispheres, in just about the center of your head.

The brain with the skull peeled off-- like a peeled apple.

Then researchers compared images of brains of people with AD/HD to the images of brains of people without AD/HD. The diagram on page 18 shows how the brains of people in each of the two groups are used differently. With this information, researchers identified the parts of the brain affected by AD/HD. The pictures show normal brains, with the bits of the brain affected by AD/HD called out.

These brain regions (and others, too) have to do with regulating attention and impulse, and with managing time. Also, some brain structures are actually smaller in people with AD/HD—on average, 3 to 5 percent smaller—not a lot, but enough to measure. Now, remember, volume doesn't equal intelligence, or people with big heads would be the smartest.

The point of all this is that it proves, scientifically, that AD/HD brains work differently. And the difference is both good and bad, after all. These differences lead to the good parts of AD/HD, such as a great sense of humor or lots of ideas or strong emotions, along with your forgetfulness or whatever symptom you have that you hate the most. Another good thing is that it definitely means that AD/HD is not your fault. Another bad thing is that you can't just decide not to have AD/HD.

Brain Paths: Prefrontal Cortex

People with AD/HD have smaller prefrontal cortexes than people without AD/HD. This matters. The prefrontal cortex is sometimes referred to as the seat of "executive function," which means it injects thought, reason, planning, and logic into our naturally impulsive thoughts and our naturally occurring emotions.

The prefrontal cortex helps to serve as brakes on your actions and emotions. Except that it works better in people who don't have AD/HD. And mental brakes are often a good thing, as you know if you have ever impulsively done something ("I wonder how far I can walk with my eyes closed before I run into something"), then gotten hurt ("Ouch. Didn't work."), or if you have gotten really upset ("Why did you yell at me? I hate you!"), then realized that you were overreacting ("Oh. To stop me so I didn't get run over by some speeding cyclists. Oops.").

This is part of the reason those of us with AD/HD are impulsive and often get in trouble—because the idea or emotion takes over before we have time to think about the action. Our brains are supposed to filter events and feelings and details, to help us focus and stay on task. Specifically, that is the job of the prefrontal cortex. People with AD/HD often skip that part. Instead, they take some shortcut past the frontal cortex, which is the part of the brain that filters all the incoming sensory data. The prefrontal cortex decides what's important, sets priorities, and helps you ignore the unimportant stuff passing through your brain. But not in people with AD/HD. Nope, to us it's all about equally important.

Imagine trying to make tea without a strainer or a tea bag. The leaves float all over the cup, and it's hard to sip the tea without swallowing extra gross crunchy bits. Or imagine trying to make coffee without using a filter—the grounds and the coffee are all muddled up.

This is an extreme example, I admit. But you get the idea.

When feelings and thoughts are all mixed up, and you can't get at the good stuff without crunching on the bad stuff, then it's like having AD/HD. Nothing is filtered correctly: it all seems equally important. You can't figure out what to pay attention to and what to ignore.

With a Filter

With a filter, school goes like this: teacher talks; you ignore both the fly buzzing on the window and the kid making the cool paper airplane next to you. That's because the filter tells you what to listen to and what to toss out.

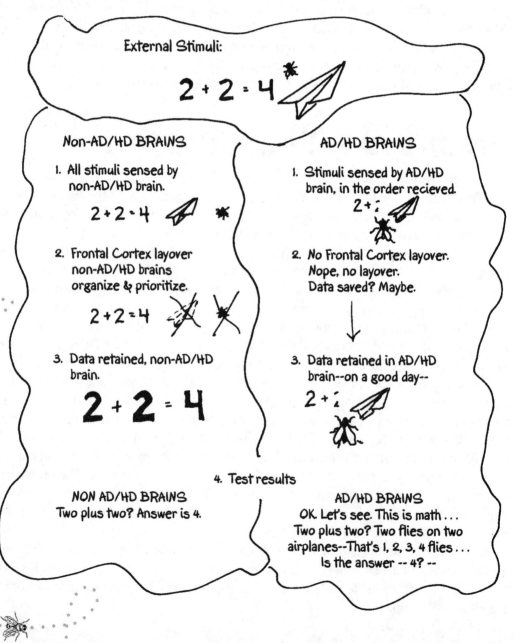

Without a Filter

Without a filter, school goes like this: teacher talks; you look at the fly who buzzes near the window where the kid is making and then launching a paper airplane, one of those cool ones that goes the distance. By now you have no idea what the teacher is talking about, and if it's on the test, you're doomed. The filter isn't working. All sensory information arrives at your brain and is processed as you experience it.

It's hard to focus.

No filter.

Memory

Memory isn't very well understood, but since a lot of the problems that AD/HD brings us result from forgetting stuff, it's worth talking about.

Using observation, scientists have defined several kinds of memory:

◎ Working memory, where you keep current information in play so you have a chance to act on it (for instance, remembering what number you need to divide by after you add up a bunch of numbers).

◎ Long-term memory, where you keep memories of your first day of school or that time you got sick in the motel room on vacation.

To get a memory into long-term memory, you have to be able to keep it around in working memory, first. Working memory usually doesn't work very well in people with AD/HD, which means that you forget things *before* you can get them into long-term memory. Things you are interested in, though, and that you think about, stay in short-term memory and then transfer into long-term memory, which doesn't seem to be at all affected by AD/HD.

Four brain regions involved with memory include:

1. the hippocampus (helps form long-term memories, which are the ones that stick in your head longer than a teacher's mention of homework assignments),
2. the amygdala (emotional memories),
3. the corpus callosum (the thick wall that separates the two halves of the brain), and
4. the prefrontal cortex, which we've already talked about.

These are all affected by AD/HD (mostly, they are smaller), which helps explain at least a little why we tend to be forgetful. Memory is also affected by brain chemistry (that's in Chapter 3).

Another thing that helps us create long-term memories is sleep. Studies have shown that sleeping helps us remember things. In one study, scientists taught a group of people a new skill. The researchers let half of this group sleep, and interrupted the sleep of the other half. In the morning, the researchers tested the entire group. Guess what? The people who slept were much better at the task than they had been on the day they learned it. The people who didn't get sleep performed worse than they had on the day they learned the new task.

Remembering and sleeping—things we're not good at. At least part of the reason people with AD/HD don't sleep well has to do with brain chemistry, which is in Chapter 3. See how all this twines together?

Memory FACTOIDS and Tip

Researchers have established that you can keep about 7, plus or minus 2 things, in your head at a time. Some researchers think the magic number is actually 4, or maybe 4 plus a few. Anyway, you can't hold many individual facts in your head, whether or not you have AD/HD.

Also, you can only keep those bits in your head for about 20 seconds before you forget the bits and new bits take their place. That means you have 20 seconds to write down whatever you need to remember. Otherwise, repeat it continuously until you find a pencil and paper, or until you can get a friend to help you remember it, or something!

Brain Geography and AD/HD

A boatload of research has been done on AD/HD. The geography part, the chunks of the brain affected by AD/HD, has been well researched, and the findings help to explain why people with AD/HD have our mixed bag of traits, the good and the not-so-good. But no one has really figured out how the different parts of the brain talk to each other. This is another area of research, and is discussed next.

The Back Page
•••

Cheat Sheet

The brains of people with AD/HD are a little different from the brains of people who don't have AD/HD—not a lot, but enough to make a difference. Also, the parts of the brain that are affected by AD/HD are the ones that are associated with common symptoms of AD/HD, such as disorganization, forgetfulness, distractibility. Scientists figured out which parts of the brain are affected by using brain imaging methods, such as MRIs and fMRIs.

•••

Ask Ms. ADDvice Lady

Dear Ms. ADDvice Lady:

I have to ask for help a lot. Like, when I lose things and forget about homework and tests, I have to ask for help, from teachers, from other kids, from my family.

I hate to ask for help all the time. And here I am asking for help from you. But this is help to keep me from asking for help. Isn't it?

Help-Full Hattie

Dear Help-Full Hattie:

Let's start with some questions, shall we? Do you mind helping others? Was that a no? You don't? So long as the people you help appreciate the help, right? Is this paragraph nothing but questions?

So, you don't mind helping others. You just mind *asking* for help.

Isn't that odd.

I, myself, also ask for help. After all, I have AD/HD. Thanks to brain wiring and other physical factors, I forget things. I'm late. I lose things. So, I may need help when these things happen. I call that being high-maintenance.

I am high-maintenance. Here's where this answer turns into a commercial: But I'm worth it.

Now, that may sound vain. But that's the best I've been able to think of. After all, I like to help others. And as this book mentions, those of us with AD/HD have characteristics that make us worthwhile people, so perhaps we are worthy of help from others. I personally think everyone has high maintenance areas of her or his life. The difference is that those of us with AD/HD ask for help perhaps more often and more openly. That means we must be grateful for help and be willing to help others. Again, these are good things.

So, I have to believe that I am worth the work it takes to be my friend and my relative.

Along these lines, I have a friend who has a rotten disease called multiple sclerosis (M.S.). He is in a wheelchair, and that is certainly one version of high maintenance. And he is a pleasure, a true and fine friend.

He helped me understand that high-maintenance has an undeservedly bad reputation. I feel lucky to know him, and happy to help him in any way I can.

So, high-maintenance is not bad. You just have to be worth it. And you are.

Ms. ADDvice Lady

• • •

Fun Facts to Forget

In the 1800s, during the Victorian era (so-called in honor of Britain's then Queen, Queen Victoria), phrenology was a "science" that was very popular. Phrenology was the study of the shape and bumps of people's heads (or their "topography," ho ho). The phrenologist would analyze your "head bumps" and then be able to talk of your intelligence and character.

Unfortunately, phrenology was discredited, so don't bother to map your own head bumps.

• • •

Chapter 3

Brain Chemistry

To understand AD/HD, it helps to know a little chemistry, but not the kind you're likely to do in a high school chemistry lab. It helps to know a little brain chemistry, which is also called neurochemistry, and is a mix of biology and chemistry. It has to do with how brain nerves—also called neurons—behave.

First off, in case you didn't know this: the brain is essentially one big chemical factory. Nerves need chemicals to talk to one another, to transmit chemical signals. Your brain says "pick up a piece of paper" and the nerves in the brain have to send that information to your hand so it can pick up the paper. They do that by talking to each other, by transmitting signals. Because AD/HD brains have chemical production problems, some brain signals don't get very far before they are sidetracked. Kind of like I get sidetracked sometimes.

Brain chemicals are called neurotransmitters. To review: all nerves, including brain nerves, need the right chemicals—neurotransmitters—in the right amounts, to transmit the latest news by way of nerve impulses.

Helen: Hey! That's another way to explain AD/HD. Our impulse control problem is a NERVE IMPULSE control problem.

That Takes Some Kind of Nerve

Nerves (pretty much throughout the body) are shaped kind of like tiny celery, except that instead of stiff stalks, they have wilted stalks. Okay, so they are like really,

really, old, limp celery. The leafy bits are the dendrites. The stalk is the axon. Impulses run along nerves, then jump from the end of the axon (like the end of the stalk) of one nerve to the tips of the dendrite (leaves) of another. So nerves are like (limp) celery stalks standing on top of one another. The nerve's message needs to make the leap between the stalk/axon end and the leaf/dendrites, and that's what the neurotransmitters do: they act like little ferry boats carrying the messages.[1]

AD/HD brains make and use neurotransmitters differently from non-AD/HD brains. Basically, in AD/HD brains, not enough neurotransmitters are available to carry the signal on to the next neuron (that is, nerve). If the neurotransmitter isn't there to carry the signal to the next neuron, the information doesn't go any farther. This is why people with AD/HD can seem distracted or inattentive—they are inattentive, because messages requiring attention don't get to their destinations.

AD/HD brains may or may not *make* enough neurotransmitters, but the brain recycles them (busts them up and breaks them down) too quickly. Many of the AD/HD medications work to slow down neurotransmitter recycling. That's right—brains recycle brain neurochemicals. This results

NERVE SIGNAL

dendrite

nerve cell(ery)

axon

neurotransmitters

dendrite of next nerve

axon

Synapse Definition

A synapse (SIN apps) is more of a "where" than a "what." It is the space between neurons, where the ferryboats haul neurotransmitters from one nerve's axon to the next nerve's dendrites. Technically speaking, the side where the neurotransmitters board the ferryboats is called the pre-synaptic side. Then the neurotransmitters diffuse (spread out) through the space. The other side of the synapse is called the post-synaptic neuron, where the neurotransmitters latch onto the receptors (the docks) of the next neuron. When enough neurotransmitters bind (or attach) to the post-synaptic neuron, the nerve fires, so that it releases neurotransmitters at its own pre-synaptic end. Repeat.

Receptors are like keyholes that only work with the right kind of key. Each receptor accepts, or binds to, one type of neurotransmitter.

---

[1] Celery and ferry boats? If your English Composition or Language Arts teacher ever needs an example of a mixed metaphor, this would be it.

in more neurotransmitters sticking around to help transmit messages from one part of your brain to another. (Researchers use the word re-uptake for brain chemical recycling. Re-uptake? Yes, re-uptake. I am not making this up.)

Neurotransmitter Introduction

The neurotransmitters that are involved with AD/HD include:

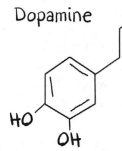

Dopamine

Dopamine (DOH pah meen): this neurotransmitter has to do with controlling impulsivity, paying attention, and memory. Dopamine is an excitatory neurotransmitter, which means it helps the nerve cells fire off impulses to communicate with one another.

Norepinephrine (NOR eh pih Nef rinn): this neurotransmitter is also referred to as noradrenaline. This is the chemical that helps you pay attention. For example, when you are in a crisis, a lot of this neurotransmitter is made available to help you pay close attention. It makes sense to pay attention during a crisis, so this is your body's way of making sure you ARE paying attention—letting loose the norepinephrine. Norepinephrine starts out as part of dopamine, which is then busted into smaller molecules, one of which is norepinephrine (which in turn is busted into epinephrine, also referred to as adrenalin…).

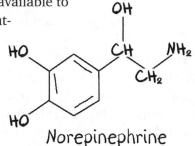

Norepinephrine

Serotonin

Serotonin (SAR-ah-TONE-in): this is involved with sleep and mood. In other words, if you don't have enough serotonin, you often have sleep problems and get depressed more easily. This is also an excitatory neurotransmitter.

GABA, which stands for Gamma Amino Butyric (GAH-muh uh-MEE-no bue-TEER-ick) Acid: GABA is an inhibitory neurotransmitter, which means it tells other neurons to stop firing off messages. That means it tranquilizes neuronal firing. In short, you relax.

Gaba

AD/HD medications help treat AD/HD symptoms by balancing neurotransmitter availability in the brain.

Neurotransmitter FACTOID: Smoking and Dopamine?

Twice as many teenagers with AD/HD smoke as students without AD/HD. It turns out that this is because nicotine—the stuff in cigarettes that makes you addicted to them—helps with focus.

Nicotine encourages the release of dopamine and helps everybody pay attention, whether or not they have AD/HD. As it turns out, nicotine latches onto the same receptors that bits of broken-down dopamine do.

This does NOT mean you should go smoke, or chew nicotine gum. Don't smoke. (Smoking is gross, expensive, and potentially lethal. And did I mention it literally stinks?)

But it does mean that research into this might result in another treatment, this one using the receptors that nicotine latches onto.

To summarize: AD/HD brains don't make and use neurotransmitters in the way that non-AD/HD brains do. And because we're short on neurotransmitters, the messages that the nerve tries to transmit don't always make it all the way down the line. A lot of this happens when nerves in one part of the brain are talking to another part of the brain. Let's take, for example, the part of your brain that has to do with remembering a homework assignment. When the teacher mentions the assignment, the information goes into your head and nerves start signaling. Before that information makes it to the hippocampus and wherever else memories are formed, another bit of information comes in. That information immediately wins, effectively wiping out the information about homework, which started traveling through your brain a second or two earlier. So, you forget stuff.

Another plain fact is that up to 50 or 60 percent of people with AD/HD have more than just AD/HD[3]. These extras can include any of your basic, go-talk-to-a-counselor kind of conditions, such as depression, anxiety, learning disorders (LD), Tourette syndrome, and conduct disorders.

Bo: Blame the neurotransmitters next time you forget to hand in an assignment. "My neurotransmitters ate my homework."[2]

Use It Before You Recycle It

Your body recycles neurotransmitters, breaking them down and reusing the molecules they are made of. It makes sense, if you think about it. Otherwise, you would have a bunch of spare neurotransmitters, some old and maybe messed up. So the body lets the neurotransmitters work for awhile, then reuses them.

---

[2] Just kidding. You still have to hand in your homework.
[3] American Academy of Pediatrics research has come up with this estimate.

But if it happens so fast you don't get to use what you just recycled, then it isn't such a good idea, and that's what happens in AD/HD brains.

Imagine that your newspaper was delivered directly into your recycling bin and hauled away before you got to read the comics. That's just as if you didn't get the paper delivered at all. That is exactly what AD/HD brains do—remove the neurotransmitters before they have a chance to do their jobs.

Some of the medications you can take for AD/HD work by slowing down recycling. These are discussed in Chapter 6.

If Two No's Make a Yes, Then Do Two Disorders Make One Order?

Yes, you might well have more than one condition or disorder, not just one.

Scientists don't know why this is, except that parts of the brain work very closely together, so that if you don't use neurotransmitters right, and neurotransmitters do more than one thing, then I guess it makes sense that you would end up with more than one disorder, by the nature of what else the brain chemical does.

Studies show that girls with AD/HD are especially likely to be anxious and depressed, so we're going to talk about those two in Chapter 5.

FACTOID: Another Type of Synapse

Until 1999, scientists only knew about neurochemical conversations between brain cells. It turns out that another kind of synapse is electrical. Specific groups of inhibitory neurons in the cerebral cortex fire using electricity and run in synchrony, which means they work together in a coordinated way. In computers, synchrony lets data travel rapidly. Scientists think that's true in the brain, too. This kind of electrical firing is another kind of synapse or nerve-conversation. That is, not only do the nerves transmit impulses using chemical ferryboats, they also transmit impulses using electricity.

Maybe some day scientists can use simple electroencephalograms (EEGs) to quickly diagnose AD/HD. That would be cool. When you get an EEG, the technician uses gunky stuff to stick little pads onto your head on specific spots. These pads are wired to a machine that records the tiny bits of electricity your brain generates when neurons fire. The whole procedure is painless, and kind of cool. And it would be great to have a quick AD/HD test, like doctor's offices have a quick strep test, so you could find out in a couple of minutes about AD/HD.

The Back Page
● ● ●

Cheat Sheet

Brain nerves talk to each other in a couple of ways. One of the ways nerves converse involves brain chemicals called neurotransmitters. You guessed it, people with AD/HD have a different balance of neurotransmitters than people without AD/HD. This imbalance can be helped with some of the medicine involved with treating AD/HD.

● ● ●

Ask Ms. ADDvice Lady

Dear Ms. ADDvice Lady:

I feel like I am a completely hopeless case, a total loser. AD/HD medications don't work for me, and I just can't keep up with my schoolwork, my chores, anything.

What should I do?

Hopelessly Yours

Dear Hopeless,

If you are SO hopeless that you are even thinking distantly about suicide, put down this book and either tell your mom or dad immediately, or call 1-800-SUICIDE (1-800-784-2433) or 911, and the person who answers the phone will help you.

If you aren't that hopeless, then good. You can try out some of these suggestions:

Have you asked your doctor if you have some form of depression, along with an AD/HD diagnosis? You might want to ask both the doctor and a parent, because depression can be treated.

Second, you need to look at yourself more realistically.

Really. Now do what I say.

Get out a sheet of paper or log onto a computer, and make a list of the things you are good at. Some good things about having AD/HD are listed in Chapter 8, so look there if you can't think of anything right away.

After you write those down (you must think of at least five, and believe all of them), then write down what you love to do. Again, write down at least five things you love to do, and watching stupid TV or playing on the computer are okay to list. You don't have to limit yourself to playing the violin or thinking about the meaning of life or other classy activities.

Third, write down a list of people who love you, and whom you love.

Fourth, every day for a week, write down every single thing you do that helps someone else, even just a friendly "hi" in the hall to some other student who looks sad.

And fifth, write down one or two things you have done in your life that you were the most proud of.

Now look these over and think about them, and make yourself think about the things you accomplish. The reason I know this can help is that I make lists like this when I get sad about having AD/HD.

This might be hard to start, but you will be surprised at how full your life is, in spite of how hard it might also sometimes be.

Keep going! Things are going to get better.

Ms. ADDvice Lady

• • •

Fun Facts to Forget

A human brain has, on average, about 100 billion (100,000,000,000) neurons.

An octopus brain has, on average, about 300 million (300,000,000) neurons.

The real question here? Who counted them?

• • •

Chapter 4

A Bad Case of Teenager Brain

Puberty, always fun, just complicates the lives of people with AD/HD even more. That problem? Brain change.

Not too long ago, researchers realized that nobody had done an analysis of what "normal" is for a teenager's brain. A teenager is defined loosely as someone gearing up for puberty (girls, that is usually when you are 11 or 12, and for boys, age 12 or 13), right through the college years.

Then this neuroscientist guy, Dr. Jay Giedd at NIMH (the National Institute of Mental Health), started taking MRIs of the brains of your average teenagers (or, if not average, at least teenagers who weren't diagnosed with AD/HD) in the early 1990s, and continued taking pictures of the same kids' brains, every two years. The results, that teenagers' brains aren't wired like adults', got to be big news in around 2000.

Anyway, scientists used to think that the brain did this one big growth spurt, from before birth up until about two years old. That was it. The rest of the time it was use it or lose it—use your brain, this is pretty much all you get. Then researchers learned that the brain keeps on changing, but still thought there was only the one big "bloom."

Scientists may have thought this because for some time it was known that, by the time you are five or six years old, your brain is 95 percent the size of an adult brain. What scientists didn't realize was that even though a lot of the brain is already formed, it continues to radically grow, change, and form new connections.

Scientists have now identified two "brain blooms." One happens at the start of your life, and another happens just before and during puberty.[1] In both "blooms," a whole lot of new brain cells grow and form new connections with one another, then some of the new cells die off.

The part that is news to researchers is that the second bloom happens, vigorously, throughout our teenage years.

As if we didn't have enough going on.

Dr. Jay Giedd of the National Institute of Mental Health used MRIs of teenager brains to reveal this second bloom. He calls this period the most "tumultuous time of brain development" since birth.

It seems the real learning occurs during the pruning part, when some of the newly formed brain cells and connections are dying off. Otherwise, Dr. Giedd points out, if size were the only thing to matter, we would be at our smartest when our brains had the most cells, which is when we are between ten and twelve years old. If that were true, things would be different. Just imagine sitting next to some eleven-year-old Nobel Peace Prize winner.

The parts of the brain that are most affected in this second bloom are these:

- **frontal lobe (prefrontal cortex):** governs reasoning, planning, organizing
- **cerebellum:** involved in physical coordination, but also adds power to reasoning skills—the coordination of cognitive, or thinking, processes. In fact, this part of the brain seems to change the *most* during the teenage years.
- **corpus callosum:** the thick band of tissue between the two halves of the brain, that help wire it so that the two sides of the brain communicate. This part of the brain is very involved in memory, and also in original thinking, creativity, and what scientists call a higher order of thinking (about humanity's place in the universe, the meaning of life and so on).

Some researchers believe that the connections that grow and develop are the ones that survive the pruning. In other words, if you are reading, brain cells that help you read get stronger. If you are doing passive things, fewer cells grow new connections. So it sounds like we should read or ride our bikes or at least take a break from the TV once in a while![2]

It helps me to know that it's hard to be a teenager for some reason aside from hormones. It also helps to realize that the teenage years are that much harder for people with AD/HD, because we get to cope with normal teenage chaos and AD/HD.

---

[1] Couldn't someone have come up with a better word for this period of time than PUBERTY?

[2] Not that TV and computer games aren't sometimes good, because they can help you unwind. But too much is probably bad. I'm looking forward to the study that tells me to eat ice cream and watch TV, instead of to eat vegetables and exercise.

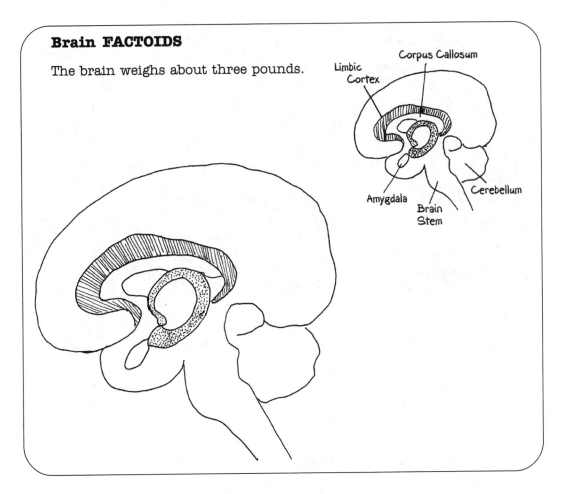

Brain FACTOIDS

The brain weighs about three pounds.

The Estrogen Component

Both girls and boys make the hormones estrogen and testosterone, although in very different amounts per gender. (Definition: A hormone is a chemical produced by one of your organs or glands that is released into the bloodstream and affects activity in your body in some way.) For girls, estrogen is puberty central AND gives us extreme emotions, including sadness and swings in moods.

Guys get emotional too. But guys make more of the hormone testosterone. Thanks to testosterone, they tend to express emotions more aggressively.

So here we are (or will be, if you aren't there quite yet) in a puddle (*or maybe flood*)[3] of estrogen, also dealing with AD/HD. Nobody knows how the hormonal surges affect those of us with AD/HD, but you can be sure that girls with AD/HD get a wild ride, given the combination of brain change, estrogen, and AD/HD.

As girls, we have a lot of emotions, regardless of the AD/HD. And because of the AD/HD, we have less prefrontal cortex development. The prefrontal cortex helps us

---

[3] Most girls enter the puberty fray between about 8 and 14.

One Study: Comparing How Genders Deal with Emotions

Remember PET scans in Chapter 2? Some researcher used them to compare how men's brains and women's brains react to something sad. One by one, each of the men and women in the study had a PET scan done. Their brains were scanned while recounting their saddest memories—some really sad things, like one of them remembered attending his dad's funeral as a kid. Both the men and women had activity in the same general place in the brain (the limbic system). The difference? The areas affected in that portion of women's brains were eight times larger. EIGHT TIMES.

In other words, when women remembered sad things, more brain real estate was affected, which indicates that women have more brain cells involved in processing emotion than men do.

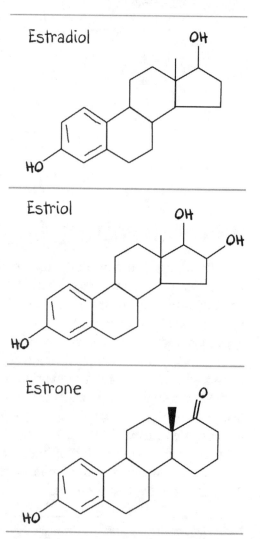

Estradiol

Estriol

Estrone

make decisions, be rational, prioritize, and control our emotions. To summarize: we have at least as many emotions, maybe a whole lot more, than your average teenage girl, and yet, less ability to control them than girls who do not have AD/HD.

Sheesh.

Hormones are clearly co-conspirators in this brain-change plot.

Women have three kinds of estrogen throughout their lives, but different amounts at different times:

1. estradiol (the one girls and women have a lot of during the years we have periods)
2. estrial (the one that women have a whole lot of during pregnancy), and
3. estrone (the one that is there all along without changing quantity much, and the only kind of estrogen that remains after menopause, except for the bits of estradiol made by fat, skin, and blood cells).

The estrogens are quite busy in the body and the brain. Researchers summarize the result of all this activity like this. Estrogen gives us some bonuses in the health category, offset by the emotional swings we experience during menstrual cycles. Estrogen also appears to increase girls' willingness to communicate and collaborate. It's as though the amount of estrogen (estradiol) reflects the quantity of emotions we endure (or maybe sometimes enjoy).

Why? Well, one chemical reason is that it looks like estradiol brings on another hormone called oxytocin, which is what women get even more of right after they have babies. Ever been around a new mother? Women are all over their babies, taking care of them.

Helen: If only we had that kind of power over our mothers, now....

Turns out that oxytocin and estrogen help girls "bond," which can be a good thing. For example, it helps girls make friends, which can help us overcome some AD/HD friendship problems. (Sometimes kids with AD/HD have a hard time making friends, maybe because our attention flits around more than others expect it to. More on this subject is in the chapter on friendship.)

Guys with AD/HD do not have this advantage in the friendship arena.

Because they make far more testosterone than estrogen, guys get muscular, get a big sex drive, and get quick and competitive in responding to whatever is going on.

Oxytocin FACTOID

When people are under stress, their bodies react. The bodies of boys and men react by increasing adrenaline, which helps them take risks and become aggressive.

But when girls and women are in stressful situations, oxytocin is also released in the brain, in addition to adrenaline. The oxytocin is further strengthened by estrogen and your basic girl hormones. That means that girls and women "tend and befriend" under stress.

In contrast, the guys are stuck with the norepinephrine (noradrenaline) related "fight or flight" reactions, since they have little or no oxytocin. The little bits of oxytocin released in male brains are pretty much erased by male hormones.

Gender

Boy brains and girl brains are different.[4] Male brains are about 10 percent larger than female brains (but remember, bigger doesn't mean smarter). Girl brains have larger basal ganglia than boy brains. Basal ganglia help the brain's frontal lobe plan and organize. Girl brains also mature faster than boy brains.

Although scientists have only begun understanding AD/HD gender differences (boy brains versus girl brains), one small difference has already been identified: teen-

---

[4] So you say, how could you *not* know that boy and girl brains are different? Good point. Even so, research tells us specifically what some of the differences are....

age girls and women with AD/HD show a reduced brain glucose (which means sugar) metabolism (which means use) compared with boys and men. That means girls' brains use less sugar than boy brains. But why? No answer to that question yet. But it is one indication that human males and females are affected differently by AD/HD.

Generally, people with AD/HD may be quick on the uptake (not reuptake, ho ho ho, a little science joke—check page 27), but, in fact, brainwaves of people with AD/HD are often slower than the brainwaves of people without AD/HD. One of the few studies on gender differences done so far shows that the pace of the brain waves of boys and girls with AD/HD are different—both are slower than non-AD/HD brains, but the girls' brain waves are twice the speed of the boys'. Again, nobody is sure what that means, but it is a difference.

One way neuroscientists study the brain is by identifying differences between brains the scientists consider "normal," and other brains. Once they identify the difference, they investigate how this difference changes behavior. This study just identified the difference, so it's a starting point for further research.

This was already brought up in Chapter 1, but remember, girls and boys display AD/HD symptoms differently. For example, girls are more likely to be day-dreamy, boys to be rowdy, and girls to blame themselves, boys to blame circumstances. It seems to me that identifying the brain differences between boys and girls with AD/HD may help explain why boy-symptoms are different from girl-symptoms.

One more thing. Research into girls with AD/HD is in its early stages, while the definition of AD/HD in the standard medical literature and textbooks is based almost exclusively on studies of boys. For example, one of the first (maybe the first?) study exclusively on girls with AD/HD was done in 2003. But AD/HD was first diagnosed 100 years earlier.[5] That means that boys' AD/HD has been researched for a hundred years more than girls' AD/HD has been researched. Hmmmmm.

What Causes Differences Between AD/HD and Non-AD/HD Brains?

So, why are AD/HD brains different? Why do the brain regions work differently in people with AD/HD, and why don't their neurotransmitters work right?

Here's the fun part: You might be able to blame your mother or your father, or at least your genes. AD/HD is largely hereditary, built right into your DNA. Researchers call this the heritability factor, and estimate that at least 80 percent of the time, AD/HD is caused by genetics. About another 20 percent of the time, it is caused by other things, like one of these:

---

[5] Stephen Hinshaw's study in 2003 looked at just girls with AD/HD. The earlier studies that included girls compared girls with AD/HD to boys' symptoms, which, as we know, are different from girls' symptoms. Kathleen Nadeau, who is an AD/HD expert who has written a ton of good books on AD/HD, says it may be the first study to focus just on girls.

⊚ things that affect brain development before you are born (that is, prenatally);

⊚ brain injury, like the events listed in the history of AD/HD, such as the viral encephalitis epidemic in 1917;

⊚ prematurity, which refers to being born too early, that is, say at 7 months instead of 9 months, so your brain didn't have quite enough time to finish wiring the brain nerves.

> **Blame Chromosome 16**
> Sounds like you can safely blame chromosome 16 for at least part of your AD/HD. Genes on this chromosome can contribute to AD/HD.

Results of AD/HD Research

Once you understand the science behind AD/HD, it gets easier to accept the syndrome, appreciate the good aspects of AD/HD, and deal with the rest. The research is moving ahead fast. Doctors and researchers are learning a lot every year.

1. Research on AD/HD supports the fact that forgetfulness and other parts of AD/HD just aren't your fault. Your difficulty in starting and finishing homework is not a character flaw or laziness, but instead, a reflection of your brain chemistry and structure. Just remember, all the willpower in the world will not alter brain chemistry.

Okay, so the "just remember" part is a joke, since remembering is the problem.

This doesn't get you off the hook. Forgetfulness may not be your fault, but it is surely your problem. You have to find some way to manage, using extra tricks and tools to remember things and stay focused. Check out some chapters later in this book for some suggestions.

2. The research on AD/HD supports the use of medication that helps make neurotransmitters available to the brain. For example, some medications (Ritalin is the one most people have heard of) help your neurons transmit messages correctly, keeping them going on down the line. Other medications (like Zoloft) increase your serotonin levels, so you're not so sad and you sleep better. Sometimes a doctor may ask you to be patient and try a couple of different medications to find something that matches your version of AD/HD. For more information about AD/HD treatment, check out pages 67-74.

3. Research on AD/HD has led to the discovery of other things that help you deal with hard bits of having AD/HD. For example, exercise can really help, because it tells your body to make serotonin naturally, which then helps you to manage your AD/HD symptoms better.

The Back Page

• • •

Cheat Sheet

Brains change a lot during adolescence. For some reason, this is new news. And if you tie that into the kinds of things adolescent girls already have going on, such as plenty of hormones, then you top it off with AD/HD, you end up with a lot of change and emotions all going on at the same time.

• • •

Ask Ms. ADDvice Lady

Dear Ms. ADDvice Lady:

I don't think it's fair that girls who already have their hands full trying to remember where they put their shoes last night are ALSO supposed to keep track of periods and THEN remember to have appropriate feminine products on hand. I can't remember what my homework from this morning was, let alone what time of the month it is.

Periodically Yours

Dear Periodically Yours,

You have brought up an excellent point. Forgetfulness and menstrual cycles are not good companions.

I have, myself, experienced this, and so feel something of an expert on the subject. Essentially, the story boils down to this: put feminine supplies everywhere. Every purse, backpack, bag, pocket, and locker. Also, it is very wise to know the location of the nurse's office at school, and to try to have some money on hand in case you need to purchase supplies.

Money. Ha ha ha, another thing to remember. I love to make jokes.

Of course, you ought to put a calendar in your bathroom and put dots on it every time your period starts, and keep a record, and pay attention to the feelings you may have unique to this time of the month, and plan and prepare.

In my case, I don't have an enormous amount of success with planning. (I have AD/HD.)

So, I prefer to cover myself in more ways than one, in this particular case, and so keep supplies in cases, backpacks, purses.... I always wonder what a male might think were he to find whatever thus equipped bag or purse I had misplaced, but then, I try NOT to wonder that. And because I have AD/HD, I can often forget what I was wondering.

Ms. ADDvice Lady

• • •

Fun Facts to Forget

Problems falling asleep, called "initiation insomnia," increase once kids with AD/HD hit puberty—it gets really hard to fall asleep for at least half of us during the teen years. Other types of insomnia we might experience include: restless sleep (just like it sounds); difficulty awakening (just like it sounds); and intrusive sleep, which is a kind of sudden intrusion of "theta waves" that literally puts you out of it—so once you lose interest in something, you might just crash into sleep (and out of your chair, if it happens when you are in class).

• • •

Chapter 5

Emotions:
Too Many, Too Often

Emotions. Too many, too often, too intense. That pretty much sums up my experience with emotions. Usually I feel like I'm standing under a waterfall, bracing just to keep upright, as the emotions dump on my head.

Bo: Having so many emotions really gets to me. I hate getting upset and angry. And I really, really hate getting into trouble, especially when I'm in trouble because I lost my temper.

Helen: I like having the good emotions, though. I am usually pretty upbeat. I mean, I have a good time a lot of the time.

Maddy: Yeah. Me too, in between the depressed part. Maybe the two are linked somehow? Like, I have to fight hard not to be sad, so when I have a chance to be happy, I really go for it.

Bo: I know what you mean. When I get to hang around with you two, I can put the worry aside and have a good time. I don't worry about what I say or do, because I know you guys are my friends.

Maddy: Three cheers for the good times!

Helen: Hip, Hip, Hooray

Maddy: I was speaking figuratively....

Helen: Oops.

The Good Emotions AND the Bad: The Prefrontal Cortex

One reason we have a lot of emotions and they all seem bigger than the emotions of some kids without AD/HD is that emotions, along with events, are supposed to be filtered by the prefrontal cortex.

Remember the example of the fly and the airplane and the math? That was an example of a person with AD/HD paying attention to lots of things equally, instead of paying attention to the important thing, math, and tuning out the unimportant stuff, the fly and the airplane. Although the fly and the airplane might be more interesting, they are not more important than math when it comes to homework and tests. Emotions also aren't filtered correctly in AD/HD brains.

Ordinarily, the prefrontal cortex helps people decide how to react emotionally, giving them a chance to think about their feelings and maybe tone down an initial emotional reaction. When people without AD/HD get angry, the anger takes a brief time-out in the frontal cortex. People without AD/HD are able to delay the anger long enough to think about whether to explode.

I, and maybe most people with AD/HD, skip the delay part and move straight to the explosion.

This is a big problem for me, and something I'm always dealing with. Right now, I am learning to wait, so I can think about why I feel what I feel, and how I should react. For example, some guy says something stupid to me. But instead of blowing up, which would ordinarily be my first, second, and third reactions, I am trying to think, "I'm mad but now that I think about it, he didn't say that to make me mad, so maybe I can make myself wait for a better time to explode." Or at least, "Yes, he said that to make me mad, but if I get mad now, I will live in detention the rest of my life. So I will explode after class and clamp my mouth shut until then."

Still, the explosion sometimes gets there before my thoughts do.

This might also explain why those of us who have AD/HD have such a good time. When good things happen, we skip the delay part and go straight to the happiness. And maybe that's where some of the creativity, the something extra, comes from, too. Maybe the time that people without AD/HD spend sorting and filtering in the frontal cortex strips away ideas and emotions that people with AD/HD use. Maybe this helps us see things differently; connect things most people don't. Also, maybe bypassing the prefrontal cortex (or just overwhelming it with quantity!) lets us go directly to compassion and empathy without pausing to even think about ourselves.

It's an idea, anyway. One that probably skipped right past my prefrontal cortex.

Another thing. When something grabs my attention, it gets all of my attention. Maybe that's because the attention skips the waiting room area of the prefrontal cortex. Otherwise, maybe the prefrontal cortex would logically evaluate where my attention *should* be focused, instead of letting me get caught up in whatever I'm attending to.

Maybe that's "the zone," as in "I was in the zone, man." I've heard that athletes and artists get into some altered (naturally and in a good way) state of mind that lets them really focus.

I love having my attention grabbed. My whole brain starts bouncing around with whatever is letting me ignore everything else.

But because emotions don't take a break in the cortex, they just keep on flowing, all intense, all the time. Because of this, I swing between emotions fast. So, I have a lot of big emotions, one after another, which is very exhausting. I need to figure out how to deal with the rapid-fire changes in mood, handle frustration and worry, and be around people where my outgoing nature (i.e., *impulsiveness*) and sense of humor are good things, not bad things.

It's hard to handle all this. The chapters on treatment talk about some things that can help you. For example, for awhile I went to a psychologist, and learned to pay attention (that joke, again) to what I was feeling so I could figure out when I was going to get upset or whatever. It's hard, and I don't always catch my overreaction in time, but at least I can catch it some of the time, now.

How Does It Feel?

"How Does It Feel?" are words from some ancient rock and roll song, which could be my own personal theme song, because everything, every little thing, has some emotional effect on me. It is so tiring and I am very, very, very, very sick of it. I hate writing about emotions, because then they get even more intense, but if I don't talk about them, how can I ever figure them out? I don't think I understand them myself, but I can describe how they affect me. Can anybody ever understand emotions?

So. I will talk a lot about some emotions, but mostly the emotions that usually end up making me feel bad.

Some of these emotions are Bo's and my own specialties, anxiety and depression. And anger, a specialty of adolescents everywhere, gets some time here, too.

One More Thing: Emotional Radar

Are you really aware of other people's emotions? Some people with AD/HD seem to be really sensitive to the emotions of others, while others just aren't and to them we are hypersensitive idiots. Anyway, I call it emotional radar, and mine is always set to high sensitivity, which can be bad because I sponge up other people's bad moods and carry them around until something else comes along. So I have to train myself to watch what I'm feeling because of other people's feelings. I'm not sure what you can do about this except talk to your counselor. After all, sometimes it's a good thing, like empathy. You can feel what the other person is feeling, and that helps you understand them and sympathize with them.

An Example of the Good Stuff: Excitement

What about the good emotions, you might ask. Well, those are pretty easy to recognize, and I hardly ever get in trouble for the emotions that I like. The best emotion, to me, is love[1].

I also like being excited and absorbed by what I'm doing, reading, or thinking. I love feeling like that. Like when I'm lost in an idea, or in writing a story, or doing improv work, and with my friends and we're on a roll, laughing and making jokes. Singing—I can get lost in that, too. I have some pals who have AD/HD and feel that way about sports.

These times are great. I feel so free, like my maniac dog. (That's maniac, not manic as in manic-depressive, which is the old name for bipolar disorder, which one of my best pals has.) So, my maniac dog is part Australian shepherd, part something else. She's from the humane society and I think she has AD/ HD. She swings between total focus and total distraction, just like me.

The excitement and freedom that I feel when I have a chance to let go and dream things up and make jokes—that kind of freedom is one of the payoffs of having AD/HD.

On to the Not-so-good Stuff: Frustration and Anger

Math is an excellent source of frustration for me. Say we're doing algebra, and I understand most of the problem, right? But I'm stuck on one part near the very, very end. So I raise my hand. When I finally get called on (waiting is like poison), the teacher answers the question but begins by explaining from the very beginning, limping slowly through step after obvious step until I could scream really loud. By the time the teacher gets to the part that I didn't understand, I can't even listen anymore because I am so frustrated and angry! I'm about to explode, crawl right out of my skin. It's all I can do not to snap at the teacher to quit being stupid and tell her to get to the part I don't understand. Sometimes I do mouth off. That's even worse. No matter what, though, even if I don't explode externally, I'm exploding internally, and that means I am not listening when the teacher finally gets to the explanation of the only part I didn't get.

By the time I cool down, we are on to the next problem or in the next class period even. By then it's too late to figure out the part I didn't get. And because the teacher already explained it once, I can't very well ask again, or at least, I don't want to ask again. I feel stupid. And on top of that, I feel even dumber when I realize that

---

[1] What about the emotion of *like*? I don't know why *like* can't be an emotion, where like is a pastel shade of love.

> "The life of the creative man is led, directed and controlled by boredom. Avoiding boredom is one of our most important purposes." —Saul Steinberg

I'm the only one who got so frustrated. Everybody else was able to sit there and tolerate the boring pace. Then I hate myself more. I still don't understand the math. I'm exhausted.

And I have to listen to another boring teacher in another class, and if I manage to pay attention and not get distracted, and this happens again.... You can see the cycle.

Then I feel hopeless. I feel like such a freak. I just don't get it. Everybody else does, but not me. Then I feel so lonely and sad. And then I get even sadder, thinking about all the stuff I forget and mistakes and mouthing off and everything.

Because I know a little about AD/HD brains, I understand that this is one part of having AD/HD—because the emotion is like a roller-coaster without brakes, it keeps getting worse. I can't stop from being frustrated, because my prefrontal cortex[2] isn't doing its job correctly, then I get more and more frustrated. And angry.

Anger. That's probably a good way to think about frustration, since frustration makes me angry. And I said I was going to talk about anger....

What Anger Is and What Causes It

Anger is a feeling that occurs when you've been provoked, or at least when you think you've been provoked. It is likely that anger evolved to help us protect ourselves from a threat, attack, or perceived threat.

So one cause of anger might be threats, attacks, or perceived threats. Some people think that anger is a secondary emotion, that first you feel disappointed, scared, or ashamed, *then* you get angry. So you might want to think about what you felt just before you got angry.

Also, thought and emotions are linked. You make an assumption, you get mad, then you think about it, and maybe you aren't so mad. [3]

Anger FACTOID

Anger isn't defined as a specific disorder or syndrome in the DSM-IV (the official diagnostic guide to psychological problems), so no one has researched anger very much. To me this is like waiting 100 years to look at girls with AD/HD. Nobody thought of this?

---

[2] Hormones, too. Let's not forget to blame them.

[3] According to Professor Jerry Deffenbacher, a leading researcher on anger and a professor at Colorado State University, "We have no DSM-IV anger-based disorders, hence there is poor epidemiology and data." This translates into: "We don't really know how many people have real anger problems."

How Your Body Reacts When You Are Angry

When you are angry, your heart races, face flushes, breath gets shallow, maybe your jaw or other muscles tighten up, and your stomach knots up. These symptoms are autonomic[4]—that is, they happen automatically.[5] Take the quiz on the right and score *your* level of anger.

What your score means

◎ 9-15: No problem with anger.
◎ 16-22: Reread this section and think about how to handle it.
◎ 23-27: Get to work. You need to start finding a way to deal with getting mad. See the next section for suggestions.

What You Can Do When You Are Angry

What can you do about it? Actually, quite a bit. The key is to figure out what works for you. As always, your first stop is talk to some adult you trust—maybe a psychologist or counselor if you have one—and of course, a book like this might help, too. Check out the treatment chapters for information on a medication and counseling. A few things you can do to cope with anger are listed below.

Think About It

Thinking about emotions is central to cognitive-behavioral psychology, one of the most effective psychotherapy methods. Because thought and emotion are linked, if you can get at the thoughts, you can get control over the emotions they generate. Think of it this way:

1. A guy runs out of a room . . . . Who cares?
2. A guy you know runs out of a room. . . . Now you care, but in what way? Don't know yet.
3. A guy you have a crush on runs out of a room. . . . Okay, you're sad to see him go, maybe? Or you are glad you got to see him before he left the room?

---

[4] That's pronounced auto (like the car) nah mick, not autognomic, for you Harry Potter and fantasy fans. Autonomic function is another brain activity.

[5] More neurochemistry. You feel this way when you are angry because your body releases noradrenaline, also referred to as norepinephrine, which also, in fact, is related to dopamine release and therefore AD/HD. (We talked about this before, but here's a reminder anyway: norepinephrine, also called noradrenaline, breaks down into epinephrine, or adrenaline. These terms are sometimes used interchangeably.)

Figure out your anger score:

Question	Answer
1. I lose my temper . . .	a. more than most people b. same as most people c. less than most people
2. When I thought I did a good job, and then get a bad grade, I get really angry . . .	a. more than most people b. same as most people c. less than most people
3. I get angry when I have to slow down because somebody else made a mistake . . .	a. more than most people b. same as most people c. less than most people
4. When I am under a lot of pressure, I explode . . .	a. more than most people b. same as most people c. less than most people
5. I get mad when I'm corrected, especially if I'm corrected in front of others . . .	a. more than most people b. same as most people c. less than most people
6. When I get frustrated, I feel like bursting into tears or hitting someone or something . . .	a. more than most people b. same as most people c. less than most people
7. People who think they are always right make me mad . . .	a. more than most people b. same as most people c. less than most people
8. When I get mad, I sometimes say mean things that I wish I hadn't	a. more than most people b. same as most people c. less than most people
9. I am angry . . .	a. more than most people b. same as most people c. less than most people

Scoring Your Quiz

(By the way, any quiz you take that is in THIS BOOK, you get a perfect score.)

Write down how many in each category, then multiply	Equals:
a. More than:_____ x 3	_____
b. Same as: _____ x 2	_____
c. Less than: _____ x 1	_____
TOTAL	_____

4. A guy you have a crush on runs out of room to talk to another girl. . . . Okay, now we have a reaction of upset, maybe anger.

The emotion of anger doesn't make sense until a lot of these facts come together. And by changing the way I interpret the facts or the events, I change the way I feel, the way I react. Logic helps me avoid an explosive expression of anger. Okay, so I might still be angry, but at least I don't explode and feel like I'm out of control. It's okay to feel whatever the emotion is. Just don't act on it before you think. Your job is to keep the feeling from running your life. And if you can get yourself to think about it, the thinking delays the emotion a little, giving you a chance to calm down a little bit.

Let's go back to the example. The emotions that you might feel because the guy you like ran out of the room to talk to another girl depend on your interpretation. If you stop to think about it, there are lots of possible explanations. Maybe he is working on a school project with her. Maybe she is his cousin. Maybe even your first guess is right and he's dating her or wants to date her. In any of these cases, does it mean anything bad about you? No. It means that your timing is bad, maybe, but nothing about you. You might be disappointed, yes, but maybe you could skip feeling angry.

Strategies for Handling Anger

Here are some ideas that help specifically with anger.

Action	What the Action Does
Breathe deeply or count to ten when you begin to feel angry.	Helps you calm down so you can think about what just happened.
Get strenuous physical activity (for example, go outside and run around the school building as fast as you can, with permission, of course).	Releases internal endorphins (a kind of built-in cheer-you-up neurotransmitter) that help you get rid of the anger.
Talk to friends or at least get away from the situation.	Helps you get perspective, understand what happened and maybe find other ways to think about it, or at least cool down while you figure out what to do. If you don't have any friends around to talk to, try to write about it. Get the feeling out, but use words, not action.
Write about the situation.	By escaping from the situation and writing about what happened, you get a chance to cool down and get some perspective.

Action (cont.)	What the Action Does (cont.)
Try using humor.	Finding something funny in the situation can help break up the tension, so that you can find a way to react that isn't going to get you into trouble.
Set up an escape hatch.	Work out a deal with your teachers, family, and friends, so that if you lose your temper you can signal that you need to get away from the situation. Agree that you will deal with the situation that led to the anger, but only after you are a little calmer. This means you aren't running away. Instead, you are actively dealing with the emotion so that you can then deal with the problem without the emotion overriding the situation.
Try using empathy.	When you are losing your temper, try to put your concerns out of the way. Try to understand the situation from the other person's perspective. This can help you forgive your own anger, too.
Use the energy of anger to the problem.	But only after you have gotten a grip on the anger and aren't yelling and exploding. The norepinephrine gives you the energy just in case the situation you are in has to do with a saber-tooth tiger. Most of the time, there is no tiger, and you have all this spare energy that needs to go somewhere and can end up as anger. When you feel that surge of energy that comes with anger, divert the energy into something useful. Then you use up the energy in a good way, instead of in a way that can make the situation worse.
Learn to watch out for signs that tell you you're getting angry—the triggers.	When you feel yourself starting to get angry, you can deal with it before you lose your temper. Again, how to do that is something I am learning to do in counseling. Check out the chapters on treatment for information about what sort of treatment works.
DO NOT: hit pillows or yell.	That actually makes you madder—more aggressive. So don't.

The Bonus Conditions

Many girls with AD/HD have what I call "bonus conditions." In books written for adults, you may see these called "comorbid" or "coexisting" conditions. What this means is that, on top of AD/HD, you have another problem with a label. The most common bonus conditions in girls with AD/HD are depression and anxiety.

What Anxiety Is and What Causes It

Anxiety is a way to say the word "worry" with extra syllables. Technically, it also means worrying lots about stuff you don't need to worry about—also called unrealistic worries. For example, worrying about a Russian satellite dropping out of the sky and landing on your head is an unrealistic worry.

Anxiety is basically a cousin of fear.

Fear itself seems to be a pretty good idea, at least in terms of evolution. After all, being afraid helps you stay alive. If you are walking outside your school after dark, and you notice a big gang of people approaching, you had better be afraid. That fear gives you epinephrine (common name, adrenaline) that translates into extra energy in case you have to defend yourself.

That instant fear reaction is a result of information sent from your senses, by way of the brain portion called the thalamus, straight to a primitive part of the brain, the amygdala (ah MIG dah lah). This same information is also sent through the prefrontal cortex, that logical part of the brain that helps you reason through what is going on.

The cortex part comes into play, for example, when you look at the gang out of the corner of your eye and realize they are a bunch of nice kids from your high school choir. Then you relax because your brain tells you not to be afraid after all. Your brain has helped you put the fear into context. Once you've figured out what is going on, you aren't afraid any more, although your heart may still be beating rapidly as a leftover from the initial rush of epinephrine/adrenaline/fear.

That same part of the brain, the one that helped you realize you didn't need to be afraid after all, is the one that can help set off anxiety. That is, the relationship between the amygdala and the cortex causes anxiety. The cortex (and the hippocampus, the part of the brain that is key to memory) helps you recall and understand elements you should be afraid of. And if you have too many of those thoughts, then you can always sense danger and be anxious about it, even when there's nothing around to be specifically anxious about.

Some anxiety is a good thing. Walking alone at night? Be afraid. A lot of anxiety about something unlikely to harm you, though, is not a good thing. Worrying about that falling satellite? Not worth the worry.

The key is to balance what you are worried about.

Sometimes, a little imbalance in anxiety happens to almost everybody. And almost everybody, at some point, does something stupid when they should have known better. Maybe they weren't afraid when they should have been, so they did something stupid, like walking in the dark alone through a bad part of town. Later, they might realize that it was a stupid thing to have done, and that they should have been afraid. On the opposite end, most people also sometimes get over-anxious about some things. Test anxiety, or maybe total terror of the school dance. Overreactions, but normal overreactions.

Anxiety FACTOID: Panic Attack

Panic attacks are brief, intense periods of fear that hit you for no apparent reason. A panic attack involves three or more of the common symptoms of anxiety, which include sweating, rapid heart beat, shallow breathing, and lots more. Typically, it peaks after about ten minutes. But you still feel bad, both physically and emotionally, after such an attack. Almost everybody has a panic attack at some point or other. So one of them is okay. Twelve of them, maybe you should talk to an adult or a doctor....

Bo: Okay. My turn. I am anxious. That's more than just worried about tests. Well, it's like that, except times ten.

Maddy: More math.

Bo: I am a pro at worry. I'll worry about not worrying, if I have to. I'll find something to worry about. Then there's your basic anxiety. Tense all the time. Waiting for the next bad thing. Not just when there's a test, either. I was shocked when I found out most people don't worry all the time.

I did okay at my old school. I stuck to routine. Teachers didn't call on me much. But then I went to middle school. Tons of kids. I get a stomach-ache just remembering the first day. And the tests! The teachers took everything so seriously. I got headaches.

I thought everybody got panicked when they talked in front of the class. I thought everybody else just handled it okay. And I couldn't find things. I would try to get organized, but then I'd forget something. One time the teacher asked for my homework in front of the whole class. I couldn't find it. I felt like crying. And my heart beat so loud I thought everybody in school heard it.

Anxiety Disorders

If you are anxious often enough or intensely enough that it interferes with your day-to-day activities (like Bo describes above), you most likely have an anxiety disorder, rather than just ordinary anxiety. People with anxiety disorders need treatment with counseling, medications, or both. There are many types of anxiety disorders, including:

◎ **Phobia:** Phobia is a fear of a specific thing. To be a phobia, the fear has to incapacitate you. Fear of spiders is arachnophobia. A fear of heights is acrophobia. A fear of enclosed spaces is claustrophobia.

◎ **Social Phobia:** Social phobia prevents someone from taking part in normal social situations. This is more than being shy. If you have a social phobia, you avoid normal social interaction because you just can't deal with it.

◎ **Obsessive Compulsive Disorder (OCD):** People with OCD repeatedly have worrisome thoughts (obsessions) that they try to deal with by repeating particular actions (compulsions). Like, if you are unreasonably worried about getting sick, then you might constantly wash your hands to get rid of germs. You wash your hands over and over, because each time you wash them, it relieves your anxiety, at least right then.

◎ **Generalized Anxiety Disorder (GAD):** GAD means you are anxious a lot. To be more specific, GAD is diagnosed when someone is worried persistently about more than one event over at least six months. For example, say you get good grades. But you worry all the time that you are going to fail the next set of exams. That's an example of an excessive worry over a long time that may be a symptom of GAD. People with GAD feel like something bad is out there waiting to happen. You're upset a lot. You don't even know what you are worried about, a lot of the time.

Maddy: My favorite is coulorophobia, fear of clowns.

Anxiety FACTOIDS

◎ Specific phobias are among the most common of all psychiatric disorders, affecting up to 10 percent of the population.

◎ Generalized Anxiety Disorder, lasting a minimum of a year, affects an estimated 3 to 8 percent of the population.

How Your Body Reacts When You Are Anxious

Here are some signs of anxiety:

◎ You feel shaky or are sweating, but not because of anything you should realistically be worrying about. (Remember that satellite?)

- ◎ You can't concentrate because you are so worried, rather than the usual AD/HD-can't-concentrate.
- ◎ Your heart beats rapidly.
- ◎ You are tense and can't make yourself relax.
- ◎ You feel sick to your stomach.
- ◎ You are afraid but you don't know what you are afraid of.
- ◎ You feel light-headed and a little dizzy.

You might get this way when you have a big athletic meet or just before you go on stage. That's pretty normal. It's having these symptoms without any real reason over a long period of time, like six months, that should make you anxious.

No. I'm kidding. You shouldn't be anxious about being anxious. You should be getting treated for being anxious. Take the quiz below and figure out *your* level of anxiety.

Maddy: Maybe you should put sense of humor on the list
of what you can do to help deal with having anxiety?

Score Your Level of Anxiety

Question	Answer	
1. Do you habitually—over the last six months—have shortness of breath or feel your heart beating fast, but for no real reason?	yes	no
2. Over the last six months, have you experienced repeated periods of panic or fear for no real reason?	yes	no
3. Over the last six months, have you had persistent pictures in your head of things you are afraid of for no reason (like getting your hands dirty)?	yes	no
4. Over the last six months, do you find that you repeat activities that don't make a lot of sense, such as checking to make sure the bedroom window is shut five or six times in a row?	yes	no
5. Do the anxiety symptoms you have sometimes make you miss an event or be late for school?	yes	no
Score the number of yes and no answers to get your **TOTAL:**	yes ___	no ___

Scoring Your Quiz

This one is easy. If you have any YES answers, tell your parents or teacher. Watch out for anxiety. You can do something about it!

What You Can Do When You Are Anxious

Check out the chapters on treatment for information about a medical approach and counseling. Other treatment methods include relaxation techniques, which you can learn from a doctor or counselor, or you can teach yourself from books or tapes. You can also exercise or do yoga, to help you let go of the anxiety.

The point is, DO something about it.

Retro Relaxation

The thirties—that's when stimulant treatment started for AD/HD, and, it turns out, is also the time when this relaxation technique was described. We're so retro.

Edmund Jacobson figured that mental relaxation comes from physical relaxation. Here's the technique: tighten one muscle group for 5-8 seconds at a time. (For instance, try to tighten all the muscles in your lower leg without actually moving your leg as a whole. This can take some concentration, if you're not used to it.) Then relax that group, and for 15 to 30 seconds, pay attention to how the relaxation feels. At the same time, imagine tension pouring out of you as your relax each muscle group.

Then move on to another muscle group. Usually, you start at your feet, then work up through your face. Hey, it works. Go figure. Even if you just spend a couple of minutes doing this, it really helps clear away the cobwebs.

What Depression Is and What Causes It

Depression refers to one or more episodes over the course of multiple weeks during which a person loses interest or no longer takes pleasure in typical daily activities. It is accompanied by four or more of these symptoms:

- Thoughts of suicide. **IF YOU HAVE OR HAVE HAD ANY THOUGHTS OF SUICIDE, PUT THIS BOOK DOWN AND GET HELP. TELL AN ADULT OR CALL YOUR DOCTOR OR 911 OR A SUICIDE HOTLINE. DO NOT DELAY.**
- Sleeping pattern changes (sleeping more or less than usual)
- Appetite and weight changes
- Problems concentrating and making decisions

⊚ Lethargy, decreased energy

⊚ Feeling worthless, guilty

Dysthymia (dis THYME ee ah) is a milder type of depression that goes on for over two years.

Women are diagnosed with depression at least twice as often as men. Not a lot of research has focused on adolescent girls. But we do know that girls with AD/HD are more likely to be depressed than boys with AD/HD. Studies show that although boys are diagnosed with AD/HD something like three times more often than girls, girls who are diagnosed are three times more likely to be depressed. Hmmmm.

> Maddy: This is the one I'm stuck with. Being sad. Feeling blue. Having zero energy. Crying way, way, WAY too much, even for a girl with too many hormones. Crying when you get up. Wondering why everybody else seems cheerful when you can't get away from the sadness. It follows you around like a puppy, except puppies are cute and there isn't one cute thing about depression. I hate it.

The good news about depression is that it has been researched a lot, and treatment can be extremely helpful.

Sadness is normal. Sadness that never goes away is not normal. That falls into the category of "watch-out." If you are sad about an event or about something that has disappointed you, that is appropriate. Sometimes this is called situational depression.

But if you are always sad and can never pull yourself away from the sadness for long, then you may have clinical depression, which is a neurological (brain) condition that can be treated. The worst-case outcome of depression is suicide. Bad idea. Never, ever the answer.[6]

Anyway, if you think you might be depressed, or find yourself thinking about suicide, talk to somebody and get help. Tell your parents, your teachers, your priest or rabbi or minister or counselor, but tell somebody right away and repeat yourself until somebody helps you.

How Your Body Reacts When You Are Depressed

⊚ You may have insomnia, which means you wake up in the night and can't fall back asleep, or can't fall asleep in the first place.

---

[6] When my English class performed *Romeo and Juliet*, my teacher talked about how Romeo and Juliet made "bad decisions." Yes. That would be one way to describe their decisions.

Okay, so almost every teenager in the world has trouble falling asleep. But if it's even harder than usual to sleep, or on the other hand, you are sleeping a lot more than usual, that's a definite clue.

◎ Your appetite changes significantly. For example, maybe food tastes like sand so you don't eat, or maybe you eat all the time, and this is different than the way you used to eat.

◎ You withdraw from things that used to be fun. If you always enjoyed *Saturday Night Live*, *The Simpsons,* and anything else showing on *Comedy Central,* but now nothing makes you laugh ever, that's a bad sign.

◎ If you find that you are avoiding hanging out with your friends, withdrawing from things you used to like to do, that's bad.

◎ If you feel hopeless or are more irritable than you can justify even using hormones and any other argument that you can think of, that's another bad sign.

◎ If you feel suicidal, go get help immediately. Put down the book, and go find somebody and tell them. RIGHT AWAY. NOW.

Take the quiz on the next page and figure out *your* level of depression.

Depression FACTOID

Four to 5 percent of teenagers are clinically depressed (that means they have a condition that should be treated, as opposed to being sad, even deeply sad, but getting over it). Adult depression affects as many as 10 percent of Americans.

What You Can Do When You're Depressed

Check out the chapters on treatment for information about medication and counseling. You can also try relaxation techniques, which you can learn from a counselor or a book (or see page 56 above), yoga, and exercise. Reading about depression helps, too. But no matter what, DO something about it.

I know this sounds a lot like what I said about anger and anxiety, which it does because they are all hooked together in your brain.

Maddy: I was really scared when I started taking pills. But it was also weird to not cry all the time. Weird in a good way. For the first time, I realized it wasn't just me being a wuss and crying too much. It was that most people don't feel sad all the time. More about medicine is in the treatment chapters.

Score Your Level of Depression

Question	Answer
1. I cry a lot more than most people seem to, and it happens a whole lot, and sometimes for no reason. (Don't count the times you cry for what you think is no reason but then your period starts, which means you were crying because of hormones, and therefore for a reason.)	yes no
2. I don't get excited even when good things happen.	yes no
3. A lot of the time, things seem hopeless.	yes no
4. I feel like a failure a lot of the time, no matter how well I do on tests or on other things that I know I can do well.	yes no
5. I feel trapped, like there's no way out.	yes no
Score the number of yes and no answers to get your **TOTAL:**	yes ___ no ___

Scoring Your Quiz

This one is easy. If you have any YES answers, tell your parents or teacher. Watch out for depression. You can do something about it!

The Back Page
•••

Cheat Sheet

People with AD/HD are often more emotional than people without AD/HD. (Part of this relates back to brain stuff.) And since some of this has to do with impatience and a low frustration tolerance, anger often crops up, on top of the rest of the many emotions you might walk around with. Further, people with AD/HD often have a little something extra, such as anxiety and depression. Girls have these two a lot. This chapter talks about some of the things you can do with so many emotions.

•••

Ask Ms. ADDvice Lady

Dear Ms. ADDvice Lady:

Sometimes at school I get so frustrated I cry. Then my eyes are all red and everybody asks what the matter is. I HATE that. What should I say?

Weeping Willow

Dear Willow:

Crying is a perfectly reasonable response to many situations, and further, other girls may well cry during school whether or not they have AD/HD. Regardless of the general popularity of crying or at the least its relatively common appearance, I agree that you may not want to explain your emotional state to just anyone.

As always, it depends who's asking how you are doing. If the asker is a friendly person, simply saying, "I got upset, but I'm okay now," is clear, unambiguous, truthful, and to the point. If the question is "What's wrong?," I would either go ahead and talk about it, or say, "I'm okay. Look, I have to get to class."

If the person asking is not a friendly person, then you may want to provide a distracting answer that isn't a lie, but also doesn't directly answer the question. For example, "I might be coming down with a cold or something." Alternatively, "I might have allergies." They are both always true, regardless of whether you've just been crying. But remember that typically the truth is your best ally, and no matter what, don't lie.

It is useful to plan ahead so that you know what you feel like answering, though.

Ms. ADDvice Lady

•••

Fun Facts to Forget

Humans have three kinds of tears:

- ◎ **basal tears,** continuously produced, providing lubrication in your eyes;
- ◎ **irritant or reflex tears,** which is the eye watering that occurs when you get something in your eyes;
- ◎ **emotional tears,** which we produce when extremely sad or happy.

Basal and irritant tears are made primarily of water and salts, with a little bit of protein tossed in. Emotional tears, though, contain 25 percent more protein than the other two kinds—and this protein is the result of stress hormone build-up. Once the build-up of stress hormones is relieved, people feel better.

One more fun fact to forget: men's tear glands are structurally smaller than women's tear glands.

•••

Chapter 6

Putting the Treat Back Into Treatment,

Part I

The things outlined in this chapter and the next one can help you deal with your life as a human female with AD/HD. The rest of this book is mostly about what you can do to get along with your family, with keeping and even making friends, and school.

It can help to have some tools to consider using. That way, you can think about which ones might help you, depending on what challenge is standing smack in front of you that minute.

Learning about AD/HD is one of the most important things you can do to deal with AD/HD, at least according to two experts, Dr. Edward Hallowell and Dr. John Ratey. These guys are two doctors, have AD/HD, and wrote the classic AD/HD book, *Driven to Distraction*.

Learning about AD/HD

That is what you are doing right now, reading this book and learning about AD/HD. Good for you!!!!! Of course, this is a fabulous book, too, if I do say so.

The more you know about AD/HD, the better you can deal with the fact that you have it. Also, knowing about AD/HD helps you handle issues that crop up because of it. So keep on reading! And while you are at it, get your parent, guardian, boyfriends and girlfriends, and even your siblings, to read and learn about it, too. The more you and your family and friends know, the more sense things make, and the better off everybody is.

In some ways, this is especially important for girls with AD/HD, since we tend to do what Dr. Patricia Quinn (another expert) calls "internalizing" the AD/HD—that is, we think it's our fault. Boys do the opposite. They often "externalize" it, so they don't feel like it's exclusively their fault. Finding out more about AD/HD can help you understand what is and is not under your control, what is and is not your fault.

Ways to Treat AD/HD

◎ Learning about AD/HD.
◎ Medical treatment.
◎ School Plans.
◎ Counseling.
◎ Complementary—a kind of treatment that might work when used in combination with other treatments and some researchers have checked it out.
◎ Alternative and Controversial—treatments that some people say work but aren't backed up by research.

AD/HD: The Diagnosis Part

If you have already been diagnosed with AD/HD, and if it was pretty recent, you might want to skip this part. And one reason it might be a recent diagnosis is that girls tend to be diagnosed late (if at all)—meaning in middle school, junior high, or high school or college or even later!

The diagram on the next page has information from the guidelines put out by the American Academy of Pediatrics (AAP). Although the guidelines were designed for kids twelve and under, the same diagnostic procedure is followed, pretty much, regardless of your age or gender. Actually, researchers have only recently established that AD/HD is a lifelong condition, and that teenagers and adults often have AD/HD and need a diagnosis, too.[1] This set of guidelines is the result of two years of study, and it's comprehensive.

---

[1] Studies on AD/HD in adults started in the mid-90s, so that's pretty new, too.

The Diagnosis Part

1. You have a problem with inattention, hyperactivity, impulsivity, behavior or school problems. Some adult notices, or you bring it up to an adult.

2. Visit a doctor.

3. Assessment: The doctor asks lots of people to fill out surveys--behavioral rating scales. These people include teachers and family members. The doctor uses survey results to determine whether you have core AD/HD symptoms and the degree to which the symptoms affect your life, and checks these results against the DSM-IV criteria for AD/HD. (For example, to earn the AD/HD badge, you have to have some number of the DSM-IV symptoms for at least six months.)

4. The assessment checks for that something extra, such as depression, anxiety, etc.

5. Diagnosis

6. Treatment using a combination of counseling and medication along with close monitoring.

AD/HD Diagnosis, Short Version

The short version is that first you and your family go see a doctor. If the doctor agrees that something might be going on, she or he starts by talking to a lot of people, including parents[2], teachers, coaches, and so on. The adults fill out a ton of surveys that have been used for a long time in helping doctors figure out whether people have AD/HD.

Sometimes you get to take a computer test, too—these are called continuous performance tests. I took a test called TOVA (Test Of Variables of Attention) which took about half an hour. It was like a boring computer game. Different shapes displayed, one after another. In the first half of the test, I clicked whenever one shape displayed. In the second half, I clicked whenever that shape did NOT display. (These don't work so well for girls, it turns out, since many girls try hard to please. Also, this just measures inattention, not the reasons behind the lack of focus.)

My parents and my teachers still filled out surveys. One of the reasons for all these tests and surveys is that lots of things can look like AD/HD, so it's important to rule out look-alike conditions. Also, doctors want to check whether you have bonus conditions like depression and anxiety, so they can treat that, too.

Maddy: I was diagnosed with AD/HD when I was in sixth grade, and you know what? It was a huge relief to know that I wasn't stupid or lazy.

Helen: For me, no big deal. I already knew I was more disorganized than everybody else. And now I knew why.

Bo: I hated getting the diagnosis. I hated having something wrong with me. It feels weird. I resent it, too. Why can't I be like everybody else? And does it mean I'm crazy? Yeah, yeah, I know I'm not nuts. But it makes me feel different.

Maddy: That's too bad. I didn't know it made you feel bad about yourself. I guess I try to think about having AD/HD as just one way of understanding some stuff about yourself.

Helen: Me, too. Oh, Bo, that's too bad! After all, AD/HD just describes something about you. I guess, to me, resenting AD/HD is like resenting being good at math or bad at French. You're born with some things you are good at, and other things you have to deal with.

Maddy: I wouldn't trade being who I am, even with the AD/HD. I like being funny and chatty and I like who I am when I hang out with you guys.

Bo: I wouldn't trade in being who I am.

Maddy: I maybe would consider trading in who I am during math tests!

---

[2] In this book, we use "parents" to mean any adults in your life who function in a parent-like role, including but not limited to grandparents, step-parents, aunts and uncles, foster parents, etc. And in this book, "family" means any of the parents combined with any humans living in your house, including but not limited to cousins, step-siblings, and other random children.

Having Two Diagnoses for the Price of One

While the doctor is evaluating you for AD/HD, he or she should also be looking for signs that you have anxiety, depression, learning disabilities, or any of the other conditions that often go along with (or mimic) AD/HD. Mostly, the first step in diagnosing these conditions involves more surveys and conversations with you, your parents, and possibly your teachers. If you have a condition that keeps your AD/HD company—like depression, anxiety—get treatment for that, too.

Treatment

According to lots of experts and doctors, the best bet for helping people with AD/HD is some combination of medication and counseling. You may need help at school, too, since AD/HD symptoms can make school really hard. All the kinds of help you can get are talked about in this chapter and the next one.

We'll start with AD/HD medication, since that helps lots of people with AD/HD.

Physician-Prescribed Brain Help: Medicine

The brain is a flexible organ, and you can help it along through medication and through counseling.

To review from Chapter 3: AD/HD results, in large part, from having the wrong balance of neurotransmitters (nerve chemicals) in your brain. The neurotransmitters that are out of whack include dopamine, norepinephrine, epinephrine, and serotonin.

Research has shown that several types of medicine can get AD/HD neurochemistry in better balance, and may be able to help you, depending on your specific neurochemistry. The drugs (also referred to as medication and medicine) help make sure your brain has the right mix of nerve chemicals at the right time. Types of medicine include:

◎ **Stimulants:** The medication type that has worked the best for the longest is the stimulant type. They are called stimulants because they help nerves fire—that is, stimulate the nerves so that they send a signal to the next nerve. These medications help balance the amount of dopamine available in your brain.

◎ **SNRI:** A new, non-stimulant type of medicine helps balance the release of norepinephrine and epinephrine (which start off as parts of dopamine itself!). This type is called an SNRI—Selective Nore-pinephrine Reuptake Inhibitor.[3]

When stimulants and SNRIs don't work, medicines used to treat conditions closely related to AD/HD, such as depression, can work. They include:

◎ **SSRI:** Depression responds well to another kind of medicine, cleverly called antidepressants. Many of the newer antidepressants boost the amount of serotonin available and are called SSRIs— Selective Serotonin Re-uptake Inhibitors.

◎ **GABA:** Anxiety responds well to medicines that increase Gamma Amino Butyric Acid—GABA. GABA is an inhibitory neurotransmitter, meaning it inhibits, or slows down, nerves sending messages to one another. If you have more of it, you are calmer. The medications that increase GABA are usually lumped under the category of anti-anxiety medications.

For around 80 percent of people with AD/HD, stimulant medicine works very well. If the stimulants don't work, you can try other medications, or alternate treatments, too. The chart on the right shows some information about a few medications, but for the real story, talk to your doctor.

A whole lot more drugs are available than this list shows, and new ones are always under development.

Experimenting with Drugs

Yeah, you may need to experiment with drugs, by which I mean working with your doctor to try more than one kind of prescribed drug if the first one doesn't work. You may need to try lots of combinations of medicines before you find something that really helps you. If you think about all the different brain parts and neurotransmitters involved, that makes sense. Everybody's brain is different.

You might need a little more of this and less of that, and you can't know until you try the drugs. That's because, although scientists understand how the neurotransmitters work, they don't have a method of figuring out precisely how much of any one neurotransmitter each brain can make, and in what brain region. And the reason there are so many drugs is that the brain has around 300 types of neurotransmitters, and each kind of medication reacts slightly differently with one or more of these neurotransmitters.

Give It a Fair Try

You also need to know that these medications may take a while to really work, from a day to a month to longer. You have to be willing to give the medicine the time it takes to actually work. If the medicine typically takes a month to really take full effect, you can't very well quit after four days and claim you've given it a fair try

---

[3] See the reuptake newspaper recycling example on page 29. Except it's the norepinephrine, not the serotonin, that's made available.

Drug	What It Is	What It Does
Ritalin® (methylphenidate)	Stimulant	Helps balance dopamine release. Helps regulate impulse control and improve organization and attention.
Adderall® (amphetamine)	Stimulant	Helps balance dopamine release. Helps regulate impulse control and improve organization and attention.
Concerta® (methylphenidate— long acting)	Stimulant	Helps balance dopamine release. Sharpens attention. Helps regulate impulse control and improve organization and attention.
Strattera® (atomoxetine)	A non-stimulant class of medicine, which is a selective norepinephrine reuptake inhibitor — an SNRI	Helps balance dopamine release in a way that helps the release of norepinephrine (a neurotransmitter that originally starts out with dopamine). Helps regulate impulse control and improve organization and attention.
Zoloft®, Prozac®, lots more	Antidepressants in the selective serotonin reuptake inhibitor (SSRI) category	Helps balance serotonin in your brain, helping you deal with emotions and depression, improving your sleep, and often boosting the good effects of AD/HD medications.
Wellbutrin® (bupropion HCL)	Antidepressant which is a norepinephrine reuptake inhibitor	Slows the neuronal uptake (i.e., slows the speed that your neurons recycle norepinephrine, serotonin, and dopamine). Helps you deal with depression and anxiety.
Xanax®, Ativan® (benzodiazepines)	Anti-anxiety medications, which help GABA, an inhibitory neurotransmitter	Helps the brain's GABA receptors work, so that nerves fire less, helping you to relax.

(unless you end up with some side effects you really hate—these are described in the next few pages).

If the drugs make you feel funny, watch how you are doing along with how you are feeling. Sometimes it helps to record how you feel in a journal. It might be that you just aren't used to being able to concentrate! If you are taking the stuff and still can't concentrate or get your homework done, talk to your doctor about stopping it and trying something else.

Another thing. If you are on a medicine that you have to take during school and you hate going to the nurse's office at your school, ask your doctor if there is some version of the medication that lasts all day. You could even bring that up at the initial visit with the doctor following a diagnosis.

And that reminds me. Doctors track how you are doing on your medication, which means you have to go see them more than usual, to check to see what's working. When you are there, talk to your doctor if you have any questions about the medicine, or if there's anything you don't like about the way it makes you feel.

Bo: Tell your parents if you don't like your doctor. Maybe they'll find another doctor. Or talk to the doctor for you.

Helen: I didn't like my first doctor, even though he was trying to be helpful, I guess. Anyway, my mom found another doctor for me to talk to about AD/HD medications. She's easy to talk to and I just like her better. That makes it easier to talk about medications and what I could try.

Maddy: I tried a psychiatrist who specialized in treating AD/HD, but I ended up going back to my family doctor, just because I liked that doctor more.

Watch for Side Effects

All medications have a range of possible side effects, which means that even if the medication helps, it may also affect another aspect of your life—usually for a short time. For example, you might sleep or eat less for awhile, or you might want to drink more water. If you are taking a medicine that goes in and out of your body quickly, such as one of the stimulants, you will just feel the side effects while the medicine is active in your body. Some kids also get something called a "rebound effect" as the medicine wears off, meaning that they feel symptoms even more than usual as the medicine leaves their body. Antidepressants, on the other hand, are meant to stay at the same level in your body twenty-four hours a day.

Your doctor has to explain all this to you, so you have some idea of what to expect. Sometimes, even if you haven't given a medication a "fair trial" you might want to talk to your parents about stopping the medication, so they can call the doctor if the side effects hit you especially hard or you *really* don't like them.

Maddy: That happened to me. I was on this medication, and I had only taken it for about three days but I was really dizzy and I hated it. My parents called the doctor, who said that I could stop taking it, and prescribed something else for me to try instead. And since I had only been on it a little while, the doctor told me to take half a dose for two days before stopping completely. Wait. I should have talked about that next instead of here, I guess!

Don't Change the Plan without Talking to Your Doctor

If you decide that a medicine isn't working, you need to talk to your doctor. He or she might want you to try a higher or lower dose before you give up on it. Especially if the med was working before, it might work again if the doctor increases the dose. Maybe you need more because you grew, or hit puberty so the old dose doesn't work any more.

Or your doctor may advise you to step down the medication. Typically, you don't want to just wake up and quit taking it. Your brain may have become accustomed to the help, so slowly stepping down the dose (taking less over a few days, for example) helps your body adjust to the medications' absence.

Maddy: Okay, like I was saying, that's what happened to me, and then I went a week before I started the new thing. We just did what the doctor said, and the side effects went away. The next one worked better for me.

Questions You Might Want to Ask Your Doctor about Medication

- How many times a day do I take this medicine?
- Is there some version I can take only once a day?
- What is this supposed to help with? How do I know when it's working?
- What side effects does this medicine have?
- What should I do if I don't like the way this medicine makes me feel?
- Do I have to take this medicine every day, or can I take it just when I need to focus, like on a day when I have a test?
- When should I come back to talk to you about whether this is working?
- Will the medication change who I am?

The Extreme Stances Are Silly

Remember two more things, except that these are extremes, opposite each other.

First, don't sit around waiting for a magic pill that will make it all go away. It's not out there. So don't assume that you will be 100 percent better and the AD/HD will be completely erased the instant you try the medication. Your brain and your body don't work that way.

Second, and on the other hand, avoiding taking medication to prove you are strong is silly, if you think about it. Needless suffering doesn't prove anything.

After all, it's just as extreme to say that drugs cure everything as it is to say drugs are all bad. Usually the middle ground is best in most things.

Medications can help. Your job is to work with your doctor to find something that can help you. Then keep on working on any obstacles that crop up, regardless of whether they are AD/HD problems or teenager problems or family problems or whatever.

Starting on Medication: That Was Weird

Maddy: It was weird to take an actual pill, when I first got them. I worried that it would turn me into somebody else, or make me feel funny. But then after I tried it for a week or so, I did a lot better in school, and wasn't nearly so forgetful. I was thrilled. School got easier. Do you remember taking them for the first time?

Helen: The medications? Let me think. I remember that my mom was more worried than me. She started me on a four-day weekend from school, so that I was on them for days before I got back to school. But to me it wasn't a big deal. It was more like having my vision tested and getting eyeglasses. Then I could see better. And when I'm running a fever, I take ibuprofen. I guess I look at it as more of a practical matter than anything else.

Maddy: Did you worry that the pills might change your personality? After I took the medications for awhile, I wondered if I was any different. Finally, I asked Mom, who told me I wasn't any different. That was a relief. I did feel a little different, being able to concentrate, but I still felt like me. I just wanted to make sure.

Bo: The AD/HD medication made me edgy and angry. So, I quit taking it.

Maddy: You? Bo, YOU got angry? I can't imagine that!

Bo: Yeah. Angry. So I don't take AD/HD meds. I take anxiety medication. Not much of it. It helps.

Maddy: I take antidepressants and AD/HD meds. Some mornings, especially when I have strep throat so I have to take antibiotics, I feel like I'm an old lady, taking a ton of pills.

Bo: I can tell when I forget to take anxiety meds.

Maddy: Me too! Except I mean when I forget to take the medication for depression, I can tell.

Helen: You know what I think is dumb? I found out that a lot of boys quit taking medication when they are in high school. Why? Just to prove that they can do it themselves? Okay, except that might make your life harder. It doesn't prove much, really, if your grades just go way down and you get hard to live with. I was friends with this one guy who was taking AD/HD medication. Then, he quit taking it, and he got a lot harder to be around.

Bo: Did you tell him to take his meds?

Helen: I almost didn't tell him, but then I realized that we weren't being friends anyway, when he was flunking and being angry all the time. And I think you owe your friend the truth about big stuff, and this was big. So I told him.

Maddy: Were you nervous?

Helen: Yes and no. He was being pretty awful to a lot of people, including me. I had been thinking about it for weeks. So he snapped at me one time too many, and I just plain told him. I was glad I did, afterwards, but it was hard. After that, he ignored me for a while. Then he started back on the medication, and he turned back into a friend.

Bo: Good for you. I don't know if I would have spoken up.

Helen: I thought about it for a long time. If one of you two stopped taking your medicine, you'd tell me why and we could talk about it. Still, I'd tell you the truth.

Maddy: I'd count on it. I need my friends to help me check out the stuff I miss. I mean, I miss more than assignments.

Helen: Me, too.

Bo: Me, too, too.

Keep Trying

Maddy: Bo, you had to change your medication, like I did, right? I had to try a few different medications until I found one that worked pretty well, and we also had to change the dose about five times, which I really hated. But it was great once I found the right mix.

Bo: Yes. I hated trying different medications. But I was relieved when we found something helped with my anxiety.

Myths and Realities about Medication

Myth. Ritalin is long-term bad for you and it stunts your growth.
Reality. Nope. Ritalin and drugs like it have been prescribed now since the late 1930s (1937, to be precise), and no ill effects have ever been found. This family of medicines also doesn't affect growth.

Myth. Taking stimulant medication like Ritalin means that you'll end up doing street drugs.
Reality. The opposite is true. Research shows that kids with AD/HD who have received treatment are less likely to abuse substances than those who haven't received some kind of treatment. This might be because the kids getting treated for AD/HD aren't tempted to try alcohol or other substances to try to self-medicate their AD/HD.

Another Topic Altogether: Getting Help at School

Some kids with AD/HD handle school okay—their grades are okay, they have ways to cope with the symptoms. Other kids have a harder time. If you have a tough time with school, you might want to talk to your parents, a school counselor, or a teacher about getting help. For example, consider getting help if you:

◎ are failing a class because you don't remember to do homework, or to turn it in if you do remember to complete it;
◎ are spending WAY more time completing homework than your classmates without AD/HD;
◎ often get in trouble at school for daydreaming or talking too much;
◎ get way more frustrated than other kids do when the teacher explains something forever or when you have to waste a lot of time doing nothing.

Students with AD/HD can get help at school through an Individualized Education Program (IEP) or a 504 Plan. Basically, the first way involves getting the school to provide you special services that cost the school extra money, and the second involves getting the school to make changes to the classroom, your assignments, or the instruction, but without any extra cost to the school.

Maddy: I think of them as savings plans, as in saving me from going under.

What Is a 504 Plan?

A 504 plan spells out how the school accommodates the student with AD/HD within the regular classroom. An accommodation is a change that is made that does not affect the content of what you are learning. Here are some examples of accommodations:

- A seat assignment closer to the front of the room, to help you stay focused
- More time for tests or a quiet room to take them in
- Shorter assignments or more time in class to work on assignments
- Someone helps you take notes

504 Plans are typically created by parents, teachers, students, and counselors. Once a year or so everybody meets again, to talk about whether you need the plan changed.

To qualify for a 504 Plan, you need "proof" that you have a disability (like a doctor's diagnosis of AD/HD) that interferes with a "major life activity," which in this case is learning. This is because Section 504 is part of a larger anti-discrimination law that requires that organizations (including public schools) that accept federal funding make sure that people with disabilities can participate equally in the organization's activities. A letter from your doctor describing your diagnosis and how it affects you is usually enough to establish that you need a 504 Plan.

What Is an IEP?

An Individualized Education Program (IEP) is like a 504 plan, because it can list accommodations to help you. But it also specifies:

1. Modifications (changes to the content of what you are learning) you need. For example, if you have dyslexia (your brain gets stuck trying to sort out the order of letters in words) in addition to AD/HD, you might have goals related to bringing your reading skills closer to grade level. (That might get you out of reading *Les Miserables,* for example.)

2. Special services you need, if any. Special services include things like speech therapy, occupational therapy, tutoring, help from a reading specialist, or counseling from a school psychologist. For example, if your handwriting is really awful, an occupational therapist might help you learn keyboarding skills, or if teachers have a lot of trouble keeping your attention, a special education teacher might consult with them about ways to help you focus.

3. Whether you need to receive any help outside of the regular classroom. For instance, if you need to work with a reading specialist, the IEP might let you get out of a regularly scheduled class for an hour a day to work with the specialist.

4. Lots of other things, such as how to measure your progress and whether you need to take a class in the summer (yeesh).

Maddy: A 504 is like a puppy version of an IEP.

What started this is the Individuals with Disabilities Education Act (IDEA). The IDEA is a federal law that ensures that all school-aged children in the U.S. receive a free appropriate public education. The Individualized Education Program (IEP) is required under the IDEA. One of the differences between the two plans is that you need to jump through more hoops to get an IEP than to get a 504 Plan. Why? It boils down to money. Since the special services you can get through an IEP cost the school extra money, the school makes sure you really need them. So, you get tested in a lot of areas when the school evaluates you for an IEP. You might get tested for any of these:

◎ health, hearing, vision, and speech,
◎ social and emotional issues,
◎ communication abilities and learning disabilities,
◎ intelligence testing, and
◎ academic performance.

To qualify for an IEP, you are tested to make sure you meet the criteria for one of the disabilities listed in the law. For students with AD/HD, that usually results in a label of "other health impairment," but you might also have a learning disability, a speech and language impairment, or something else, if AD/HD is not the main condition affecting your learning.

Having a 504 plan or an IEP does NOT mean you're dumb. You know that, right? Nobody would think a kid who was blind was also stupid because that kid had to learn Braille, so why should it be dumb for you to have to learn in ways that help you handle having AD/HD? I had to get over feeling, or thinking, that I was dumb because I got some help.

Helen: I know some kids who are in the honors program and have AD/HD and an IEP. That makes sense. AD/HD and dyslexia, the disorder that has to do with having a hard time reading, don't have anything to do with your IQ. Just with some brain wiring.

Maddy: My mom set up a 504 plan for me at school, in the middle of last year. The plan helped because it sets out some ways the teachers can help me, since I come as a package of the good, the bad, and the twitchy.

Bo: I have an IEP. Special education. At first I didn't want it. I'm not stupid. I cried when I found out it was special education. Then I found out that it only means help. I wish I didn't need it. I wish I didn't have AD/HD. But that's a waste of time. So I quit thinking about that.

Helen: Not me. I don't have any plans. I think that's because I have better camouflage than you other two.

Bo: Helen, your camouflage is good, not perfect. I know. Call me Detective Bo. I've seen your locker.

Helen: You've seen my locker? How'd you find it under all that stuff?

The Back Page

•••

Cheat Sheet

To begin to deal with having AD/HD, first of all, you need a diagnosis, then you need treatment, and you need to get used to the idea that you have AD/HD. After you get a diagnosis, you have choices about what can help you out. Medication sometimes works. Also, you might want to see if you want to go for some kind of plan to give you some help at school. After all, you've got your hands full with the AD/HD, so you're already plenty busy. THEN you add school, which means you need to be everything AD/HD can make hard: focused, conscientious about time and homework, and more. So it makes sense that schools would work out some kind of deal to help the kids with AD/HD.

•••

Ask Ms. ADDvice Lady

Dear Ms. ADDvice Lady:

What do I say to people when I get called out of class for some IEP or 504 thing, or have to go to a doctor or counselor appointment during the day?

The Alphanumeric Kid (I5E0P4)

Dear Alphanumeric Kid:

I never before noticed that the plans are all numbers and letters, so you have already brought up an excellent point. Given that, I now know that you are more than just a number in the system. I mean, really. Look at all those letters!

I digress. (I am, after all, the ADDvice lady, with plenty of ADD, and AD/HD naturally, to go around. So I digress at my discretion.)

More to the point: you have these options, to explain why you are called out of class:

1. Say, "I sometimes get some help with homework." (The truth. Even if you are leaving class to go for counseling or something, all of that ultimately helps with homework. And, this is something no one is likely to ask you any more about. If someone asks further, talk about AD/HD.)

2. If the person asking is no one you know, simply say, "I have an appointment."

3. If the person asking is your pal, you can roll your eyes at her.

I would like to pause here, and say that telling the truth has many unbeatable advantages, so long as you are not talking to people likely to bully or harass you later. If the question asker is neither of the above, a lot of good can come from briefly informing the asker about AD/HD. Sometimes you learn about them and their troubles, or at the very least, help dispel myths about AD/HD.

Ms. ADDvice Lady

•••

Fun Facts to Forget

"Write it down" takes on a new meaning. This may not only be key to remembering homework assignments but it may also tell you if you have AD/HD in the first place. A study currently underway is examining whether the typical rotten handwriting of those of us with AD/HD can be analyzed in a way that indicates whether the writer has the disorder or not.

This study uses equipment that analyzes 205 points per second, with a resolution of 0.01mm. (That's small.) No word yet on success of this experiment. Sure would speed up the diagnosis process outlined earlier in this chapter. The diagnosis would go something like this: Write your name.

•••

Chapter 7

Putting the Treat Back Into Treatment,
Part II

Counseling

The second part of the doctor-recommended way to deal with AD/HD includes counseling, which does not mean lying on a sofa somewhere talking about your dreams. It does mean finding somebody to talk to who can help you deal with some of the not-so-good stuff of having AD/HD.

Maddy: If you are willing to give counseling a try, make sure you like the lady or the guy. One person I went to, I resented. A guy. And I went to a lady I liked a lot, even though I didn't much want to go. I got some stuff out of it, but I'm not going right now.

Helen: It's really nice to have somebody to talk to, depending on the kind of person you are.

Bo: Not me.

Helen: That's why I said depending.

I bet that a bunch of kids you know are already seeing counselors. Even if they don't advertise it. And I also bet that a bunch of kids you know are taking some kind of medicine. Even if they don't advertise it.

The reason I know this is that when I mentioned to one friend that I was seeing a counselor and had AD/HD and was taking medicine, she told me her story, and on and on. Then I ran into another kid while waiting in the counselor's office. And once I started talking about it a tad more openly, I heard a lot of things from a lot of people.

Counseling or Shrinking or Psychotherapy

Counseling is talking to somebody about your problems and concerns, and finding better ways to deal with them. The short version of why to go to counseling is that it can help you deal with your life. Living is hard. AD/HD can make it harder. Then toss in being an adolescent female. Well, let's just say it can feel like a whole lot is going on.

Counseling helped me deal with daily things, like how hard it is to pay attention. It also helped me deal with anger and the other emotions that can engulf me. Like, I hate getting in trouble for forgetting homework, and the chaos in my life in general.

Pick a topic, any topic. The stuff that bugs you, you can talk to a counselor about. It's funny how much it helps to have somebody on your side who listens to your problems, takes them seriously, and talks to you about problems, feelings, family, and friends—whatever is hard for you. And the counselor can also talk to you about family sorts of problems. Sometimes the counselor will even work with your parents and siblings, too, to help your family deal with AD/HD.

Counseling helps me feel more like I have control over my emotions and my life. Instead of being ambushed by rapid-fire emotions, or feeling like a misfit or a loner, I learned some ways to handle whatever is hard.

Let's just talk about these two things: emotional ambush and feeling like a misfit.

After I started going, I learned to sometimes catch myself before I exploded. I also realized that I felt like a misfit because I interrupt a lot and miss out on some social signals. So the counselor helped me learn how to relax, how to notice when I was going to be ambushed,[1] because usually there are some signals. Then I learned what to do when I catch the signals.

Anyway, going to counseling was like a shortcut in figuring out how to deal with some hard things about living. It felt sort of like combing my hair—it was tough when there were knots in the hair, but it was so soft once I got it brushed, then combed out. Counseling helps me get unstuck, to figure out better ways to deal with problems.

---

[1] The counselor said the signals are different for everyone. I learned how I feel anger. It sort of rises up from my mid-section. It took a while, but thanks to the counselor, I started trying to remember what I felt like just as I was getting angry or upset. Once I caught on, I could try to deal with it before the tornado of emotions struck.

We all have ways to deal with things. It's just that some of them may not be working very well.

For example, you can deal with the explosion issue, the emotional ambush issue, by sort of disconnecting, so that you don't feel anything. It works, but it's got some pretty ugly and serious side effects, like never feeling happy, along with never feeling upset. To me that's a bad trade-off.

So back up. Let's talk about finding a counselor, what happens, the whole thing.

What Training Does a Counselor Have?

The hard thing about finding a good counselor is that pretty much anybody can set up shop and say that he or she is a counselor. It's not like being an MD, where you know the doctor has gone to medical school and passed a national medical exam.

So it's important to find out how the person trained as a counselor. Here are some of the kinds of specialists who have trained in the field of psychology:

Psychiatrist: A medical doctor (physician) who specializes in diagnosing and treating conditions that affect people's thinking processes or emotions. Often this is the kind of doctor you visit to figure out what medications to try. Sometimes they do the talking kind of counseling, but mostly they focus on medical treatment of AD/HD.

Psychologist: A professional who majored in psychology in graduate school and got either a doctorate (Ph.D. or Psy.D.) or a master's degree (M.A.). Psychologists can't prescribe medications, but do the talking kind of counseling with individuals or groups. Psychologists are also qualified to do intelligence and achievement testing, so one might be involved in diagnosing your AD/HD.

Psychoanalyst: Someone who a college degree who attended a specialized institute teaching a specific kind of analysis, such as Freudian analysis. (Sigmund Freud is the guy with the beard who invented psychoanalysis, which cartoonists like to draw with patients lying on a sofa talking about dreams.) In some ways, he helped start up the practice of counseling, but going to a psychoanalyst is picking someone who might be trained with a narrow focus.

Social Worker: A professional who has a bachelor's, master's, or doctorate in social work, which involves helping people do better at getting along in the world (such as school). Social workers can have all sorts of specialties, such as hospitalized children, or retired people, or teenagers who have gotten in trouble with the law. You probably would want one who has worked with other kids with AD/HD.

Lots of other people practice counseling, maybe with a degree in education or something. Be careful picking out a counselor.

How Do I Find the Right Counselor?

To get counseling that works, you need somebody you feel comfortable with. Trust your own sense of whether you like the person, or feel like you can talk to the person. That's one of the biggest things you have to have to make counseling work. If you feel indifferent toward the counselor, or worse, you don't much like him or her, you will get nowhere. What a waste.

You probably also don't want to pick a counselor who patronizes you, seems like he or she is judging you, doesn't listen to you when you try to talk about a problem, or who acts like they know more about you than you do. (Of course, you probably wouldn't like any counselor who did these kinds of things, anyway.) My mom asked around to find out whether her friends could recommend any counselors. Then we checked out their credentials and interviewed them, which I hated and made me really uncomfortable.

During my first few months of counseling, my mom asked me whether I liked the counselor. If your mom or dad or the counselor doesn't ask you that, tell a friend to check in with you so you actually think about whether you like the person and whether you feel you are figuring a few things out. That's kind of vague, but again, it's feelings we're talking about, not yes and no questions like whether the water is frozen or the dog is sleeping. It seems to me that most of life is in between yes and no, perfect and awful.

What Do I Do When I Visit a Counselor?

You talk. But it isn't a "what'd you do today" talk. It's about what you feel and think, what happened and how you feel about it, and other things that make you ask questions about your life, your beliefs, and the way you and others act. The counselor might ask you questions or encourage you to bring up topics you want to talk about. He or she might suggest things for you to try doing differently, or help you come up with your own ideas of things to try. The counselor might also teach you relaxation techniques or anger management techniques or help you understand how to read people's cues, if that is something you need help with.

The part I like is the bit when I've talked to the counselor about something, then suddenly I see something in a new way, when I have an insight into why I do something I often do, or why somebody else reacts the way they do. That's the goal of counseling— figuring things out. And like I said, it's like fast forwarding the kind of thinking you might already do about yourself and life, the universe, and everything.[2]

Interview Questions You Might Ask a Counselor

◎ What kind of therapy do you do, and how does it work?
◎ After we start working together, can you tell me how long you think we need to meet and what our goals are?
◎ What kind of things have you studied?
◎ Have you worked with a lot of adolescent girls with AD/HD?
◎ Why did you become a counselor?
◎ Do you like working with AD/HD kids?
◎ How long have you been a counselor?
◎ Where did you train as a psychologist?

Will the Counselor Rat Me Out to My Parents?

No. Your therapy sessions are private. Before you even go to your first session, your parents will probably sign a form agreeing that what you say to the counselor will be kept confidential. (The only exception: if you say something to the counselor that makes him or her think you are in danger of hurting yourself or others, your parents need to be informed.) If you even suspect that your sessions aren't private, consider going to another therapist.

Now, expect the counselor to occasionally talk to your parents. Parents need to know whether you are making any progress, so they can help decide whether you need additional or different treatment. Making sure you are making some improvement might be especially important if you have depression or anxiety on top of AD/HD. Your parents' discussion with the counselor typically goes along the lines of "What can I do to help my kid?" not questions like "And then what did my daughter say about me?" Sometimes the counselor might ask to meet with your whole family in a counseling session. That makes sense, if you think about it, because part of what you are dealing with is your family. This might be especially important if you are having problems getting along with your family. But you don't have to agree to do that, if you don't want to.

Group Therapy—What's That?

Instead of, or in addition to individual counseling, some girls with AD/HD go to group therapy. It's when you and a bunch of others, usually other kids dealing with the same kind of problems, talk to a counselor, all at the same time. The counselor

---

[2] Thank you, Scott Adams, for the phrase, "life, the universe, and everything." He wrote great books.

might ask questions to get you all talking or members of the group might bring up topics that they want to talk about. As you can imagine, it's more general than talking one-on-one. It's a different way to get help. You get to hear how other people deal with the same kinds of things you are dealing with. And you don't feel like you're the only one, either, so that's good.

The counselor is there to keep the discussion moving along in ways that can help the most kids—the therapy part of group therapy, the helping part that this person is trained in.

If you have a hard time talking in a group, or if you don't feel like you can bring up some issues in front of other kids, though, group therapy might not be the best pick.

Sometimes it might take longer to feel like you are making progress, too. But that makes sense, if only because the time you spend with the group is less focused on your specific problems and the things you are trying to figure out. On the other hand, because it's a group, things might come up that you wouldn't have thought of, or other kids will bring things up, so there's less pressure to share your thoughts.

AD/HD Support Group—What's That?

A support group is not group therapy. It is getting together with other kids with AD/HD and talking about experiences, feelings, family, whatever. Sometimes this is led by a professional, but sometimes not. Like in group therapy, it's interesting to hear how other kids deal with stuff. It can sure take care of the feeling of being a misfit, because you are around others fighting the same battles you are. And it can be a big help, to talk to other kids who know what you are going through, and you can help them, too, which is a great feeling. But because there may not be a trained professional guiding the group, the focus is looser and the goals can be much more casual. It might end up being more socializing than therapy.

Are You Nuts If You Go See a Counselor?

No! See life is hard, page 80. Let's review:

1. You already have something going on with your biology or neuro-chemistry or whatever you want to call it.
2. It takes brains and bravery to deal with AD/HD and the fall-out from having it. In some ways, your first impulse might be to run away from it, or to pretend you don't have it, or maybe just choose to ignore it. And that doesn't get you anywhere. Going to counseling gets you somewhere.
3. Because this is the way you are wired, you might need some help. I bet you would think somebody with a broken leg was stupid if she didn't go to the doctor's office. So what's the difference? You've got something going on, so you need some help, so go get it!

Bo: I felt nuts.

Helen: How about after you went for awhile?

Bo: It took a few visits, but then I didn't feel nuts any more.

Helen: Why?

Bo: Because we were talking about things I was thinking about anyway. And anyway, I knew I was different.

Helen: Everybody's different, you know that!

Bo: Not everyone goes to a counselor.

Helen: I think maybe they should. I think living is hard, and that most of us need help somewhere along the way. Even if you don't have AD/HD.

Bo: You do?

Helen: Yes.

Bo: Hmmm.

Coaching

AD/HD affects an awful lot of your life. Because it is so pervasive (that is, because it affects so much of your life!), another kind of help has become available in the last ten or twenty years: coaching.

This is a good idea, I think. Some problems we deal with aren't things that counseling helps. For example, forgetting you have to write a paper is something you could talk about in counseling, because of the way you feel when you forgot to write it. But helping you get that paper written? That's where coaching comes in.

A coach is somebody who works with you, one-on-one, to help you structure your life and come up with new ways of remembering the boring day-to-day stuff you need to do. A coach can hand right back to you the control over your life that sometimes you don't seem to have.

AD/HD coaches can help you in lots of areas. In fact, the Attention-Deficit Disorder Association (ADDA) put out some guidelines AD/HD coaches may follow when coaching people with AD/HD. Some of these suggestions make a lot of sense. For example, coaches can help you:

◎ Learn about AD/HD, so you can continue to figure out how it's affecting you and lose that feeling that what's going on is a character flaw instead of a symptom of AD/HD neurochemistry.

◎ Figure out how to stand up for yourself and get the help you need, and when to talk to teachers or family about problems.

◎ Feel as if you're getting support and encouragement. Is there ever enough of that?

◎ Maintain focus on bigger goals. For example, if your goal is to get into shape, the coach might ask you about whether you are going to work out, and how.

After all, if our brain lets us forget things and lets our focus drift, then we need to find a way to remember things and stay focused, and we can't necessarily count on our own brains. That's where the coach comes in.

Coaches work in different ways. Some are very hands-on and help you organize your binder, your locker, or your room, or figure out which step you need to do when in order to finish your science project in time. Sometimes you can work with a coach over the phone or via email daily. Sometimes you meet with your coach in person.

To choose a coach, you need to do a lot of the same kind of checking that you do when you pick out a counselor. Find out if you like the coach, make sure you know what your goals are, and check the coach's credentials, especially knowledge of AD/HD. There are no formal educational requirements for coaches—they can be teachers, social workers, college students, etc. Lots of AD/HD coaches actually have AD/HD. After all, nobody understands AD/HD problems better than somebody who is living with it.

Questions to Ask a Coach

◎ What is your coaching style? What are you good at doing as a coach? Structure? encouragement? patience? direct approach?
◎ Have you worked with someone my age before? How many kids?
◎ Where did you learn how to be a coach? How long have you been a coach?
◎ Here's an example of something I need to deal with. Just briefly, can you tell me some ideas of how you would take the lead in helping me?
◎ Can you think of something you wish people would ask you but never do ask you?

Maddy: For a while, my homework coach was my next-door neighbor and friend who is a year older than I am. My mom paid her a little and I got to hang out with my friend (She was born organized, I swear. She must have had some essential genetic organizational material that I am clearly lacking.) Anyway, we'd do homework together, and she helped me get my backpack organized. I liked working with my friend more than getting nagged by my mom, although it was a little like having a tutor, except this one tutored me in neatness instead of math or French.

It turns out that people with AD/HD make good coaches, because we understand organization and AD/HD-type problems. It's easier to help someone else than to do it for yourself. Have you ever noticed that cleaning someone else's room isn't nearly as annoying as cleaning your own room? Even cleaning your own room can be more tolerable, even fun, when you have someone to talk to while you clean. For example, you can talk to the coach while you tackle piles, homework, and backpacks, instead of sitting in your room, immobile and overwhelmed, staring at your own mess. Maybe you could trade with another AD/HD kid, and help each other.

Using a coach is common sense to me. If you need help organizing and making sure you get things done, then this is a good way. It's personal, supportive, and helps you do what you're not so good at: focus!

Helen: You mean, then you both could stare at someone else's mess?

Maddy: I can just see myself sitting with you, and both of us staring at whoever's mess is in front of us! That's pretty funny . . . but, I really think we'd get stuff done, just because both of us have a good time. It's easier to help someone with their mess. I get sick of my own mess.

Bo: My piano teacher has AD/HD. She's an AD/HD coach, too. She gets it when I feel overwhelmed. She's had a big trouble with money. That makes sense. Money is like math plus impulsivity. She said she has a money-coach now.

Maddy: I want to try a coach, maybe when I get to college. Lots of adults with AD/HD use coaches. My dad has AD/HD, and he needs one, which is, I guess, the job my mother has, coaching my dad. Adults have all kinds of coaches and buddy systems they can use.

Exercise

Okay, I admit it. I am not much of an athlete. But I do like being in shape. Once our school class took a week-long camping and cycling trip, and I really liked it, even if I was tired and scummy by the end of the week. I think it was fun because I was out with friends and we were goofing off while we were riding. I barely even noticed that I was getting exercise!

Research shows that exercise, even just walking your dog for half an hour, releases a bunch of neurochemicals (they are called endorphins) that help you feel better.

Some people with AD/HD use exercise to help them focus, to be less hyperactive. Even walking gives you that kind of benefit—any exercise helps. Of course, maybe you don't need to run a marathon just before bed. That would just keep you up!

Anyway, give exercise a try. And that means more than going for one walk or one bike ride. You have to stick to it for a couple of weeks. You can always try to get a buddy to exercise with.

If you pick a buddy with AD/HD, though, watch it, in case you BOTH forget!

Helen: Exercise really helps. I don't understand why some people don't like it. After you exercise, you feel great, your mind clears up, and you relax.

Biofeedback

Biofeedback is a treatment that some girls with AD/HD try in addition to medication or counseling. Some scientific research supports its effectiveness, although not all AD/HD experts believe it is helpful. Biofeedback (also known as neurofeedback or neurobiofeedback) is pretty cool. You get hooked up with some equipment that tracks brain waves (it's called an electroencephalogram, or E.E.G.). Some of the other equipment tracks muscle action, breathing, and pulse. The equipment converts the information it gathers into some form you can see or hear. For example, with EEGs, you watch your brainwave patterns on a monitor. Then you try to control the pattern that shows up. For example, the equipment might display how your brainwaves look when you are memorizing something—when you are focused. Then you try to match that pattern. The theory is that if you could figure out how to make your brain make that pattern on command, you could command it to behave that way when you knew you needed to pay attention.

You have to go for months with this one, and the changes are pretty subtle, but some people really like it and think it really works.

Unsupported Alternative Treatment

You need to be careful when you consider using other kinds of treatments that aren't discussed in this chapter and the previous one. When you try treatments that aren't scientifically proven, you risk wasting lots of time and money, could wind up struggling unnecessarily in school if you stop your medications or counseling, and could be disappointed in wasted effort, too. Mostly, use common sense, such as finding out how the person giving the treatment learned about it, what your doctor thinks, like that. Also, if advertising for this treatment claims it is a "miracle," be careful.

Here are some treatments that so far are unsupported much or at all by research.

- ◎ Dietary plans, like the Feingold diet
- ◎ Removing sugar from the diet (I'm glad I get to enjoy some sugar! Oatmeal without sugar?)
- ◎ Chiropractic treatment involving moving your spine and head around
- ◎ Megavitamins (which means a super dose above the amount recommended daily)
- ◎ Amino acids
- ◎ Essential oils
- ◎ Hypnosis
- ◎ Anti-motion sickness medicine

You should be especially careful if you are considering trying any herbal remedies, because some of these don't interact well with prescription medications. ALWAYS check with your doctor first if you want to try some new natural or herbal supplements.

The Back Page
•••

Cheat Sheet

Aside from medical help and school help, you can also get some support for the rest of your life, too. Counseling is like that; it can help you deal with all those emotions common to many of us with AD/HD. Sometimes people with AD/HD have coaches, too, which I think of as human-planners. They are way more interesting and easier to keep track of than a regular school planner. Also, a lot of other options are out there, and some might work for you. There are a ton of options, so research carefully before trying any kind of alternative treatment.

•••

Ask Ms. ADDvice Lady

Dear Ms. ADDvice Lady:

I think this book is full of hooey. My dad says that AD/HD was just made up and that I don't have anything wrong with me, even though my mom took me to the doctor and I was diagnosed with AD/HD. I think my mom and that doctor are full of hooey, too.

Then my mom gave me this book, so I am writing you.

Hip Hip Hooey

Dear Hooey,

Oh. I wish you luck.

It's a shame that you and your dad are convinced that AD/HD doesn't exist.

Please let me know how you interpret the scientific evidence regarding AD/HD, such as the research studies that have demonstrated brain function and volumetric differences, along with studies showing the efficacy in treating AD/HD with certain medications.

And I do hope that sometime you will rethink your position on AD/HD, and be kinder to yourself and others with a diagnosis of AD/HD, and get a little help when you need it.

Ms. ADDvice Lady

•••

Fun Facts to Forget

Girls (and boys) with AD/HD have problems sitting still. It turns out that the "not sitting still" is different in kids with AD/HD than in kids who don't have AD/HD. So another method of distinguishing kids with AD/HD from other kids who also don't sit still is to map the kind of movements we make! Some Harvard researchers have tracked the movements of kids (with and without AD/HD) with two kinds of equipment (one is a thing you wear, like a watch, that tracks movement, and the other involves wearing mirrors that reflect infrared signals). Sure enough, researchers can distinguish the movement patterns of kids with AD/HD kids, compared to movements of kids without AD/HD, even those who have symptoms of other conditions that could maybe be confused with AD/HD, such as kids who are depressed or are traumatized in some non-AD/HD way.

One more fact to forget: Girls with AD/HD move as frequently as boys do, but only cover one-fourth the area that boys do.

•••

Chapter 8

The Good Stuff

"One of the advantages of being disorderly is that one is constantly making exciting discoveries."   —A. A. Milne

Nobody ever seems to talk about the good parts of having AD/HD, so I am going to. First of all, having AD/HD helps you be different. Different is good, not bad, contrary to what you might experience in your school.

Some of the best ways to be different are to be funny, to have a new or different outlook, to be empathetic, or to have that something extra. Well, you've got that if you've got AD/HD.

"In order to be irreplaceable one must always be different."
—Coco Chanel (1883-1971)

And remember, different doesn't mean alone. You need to find friends who appreciate you—people you like. The odds are pretty good that you already have some things going for you that you can directly attribute to AD/HD. If you can look beyond the unnatural world of school, you can see some bright spots.

Think about schools: at what other point in life are you stuck in a situation where:
1. You are only with a small group of people your own age.
2. You have stuff you're supposed to do and places you're supposed to be, like clockwork, between 7:30 a.m. and 4 p.m., or whatever your schedule is.

3. You have homework and your efforts are always being measured on a scale of 0-100.

4. You have to ask permission to go to the bathroom!

When you get a job, you can go to the bathroom when you need to. Your work is not graded on some arbitrary scale. You get to be around lots of kinds of people who are different ages. And you have at least some flexibility with your schedule. If you find something you really like doing, you often end up with work circumstances that let you do your best.

The psychiatrist who prescribes my medications told me that a lot of her adult patients don't need the medications as regularly as school kids do, because after you get out of college you can work on what interests you. I like this idea.

It's also a little scary, because how am I supposed to know what I want to do, what kind of work I'm going to love, when I am old enough to work? But then, freedom is scary if you think about it, and I wouldn't trade being free.

So what are these great things you might have that come along with AD/HD? Here's a list:

(Reread This Often) People with AD/HD Often—
- ◎ Have a kind of interpersonal charm or "something extra"
- ◎ Have a lively sense of humor and play
- ◎ Are intelligent or clever in some area
- ◎ Can engage fully, focusing intensely on any subject that they find interesting
- ◎ Are empathetic and compassionate
- ◎ Are creative or connect facts and observations in original ways
- ◎ Have a deep love of nature and animals
- ◎ Have lots of energy
- ◎ Are full of ideas
- ◎ Are passionate, persistent, and strong-willed about whatever they love
- ◎ Are loyal
- ◎ Are articulate and ready for conversation
- ◎ Are spontaneous
- ◎ Are quick to forgive
- ◎ Are honest
- ◎ Are lively and interesting, and never dull!
- ◎ Are resourceful, able to come up with unusual solutions to problems
- ◎ Respond with enthusiasm to new situations

So prove it, you say.

Okay. Some famous people diagnosed by AD/HD experts and physicians with AD/HD, include Thomas Edison (invented the light bulb and a lot of other things); Winston Churchill and John F. Kennedy (two great political leaders); and Albert Einstein (the theory of relativity guy, $E=mc^2$). I am also going to mention Claude Monet (a famous Impressionist painter) and Amelia Earhart (an aviatrix or woman pilot).[1]

There are more, too, and there are probably lots of women, too, except that history tends to ignore what women do, so they don't get the same attention as men get, or at least, not until recently!

This chapter is going to talk about dead famous people, mostly because when you talk to adults, the adults will know about these guys and it will make you sound smart. Also, this is the kind of stuff that shows up on history tests, so you might get some additional mileage out of knowing about them. Plus, these are interesting people. And not only did these people have AD/HD, but it was the AD/HD itself that helped them be so successful.

Thomas Alva Edison

I like Thomas Alva (what kind of middle name is that?) Edison's mother, Nancy Elliot Edison. When Thomas Edison was in second grade, his teacher said he was addled, which is an old-fashioned word for nuts. Nancy Edison, who had taught school herself, told this teacher that her son, whom she called Little Al, was extremely bright. Further, she told his teacher that she would show what you could do with such a brainy kid. With that, Nancy Edison snatched him out of school and home-schooled him. Then he became an incredibly prolific, that is, productive, and famous inventor.

Everybody with AD/HD deserves someone in their lives who believes in them. Thomas Alva Edison, who invented a lot of things, including the light bulb, was lucky to have his mother. If nobody believes in you, find somebody. If you look around, you'll probably find somebody who is rooting for you: maybe an aunt or uncle, or even an older sibling, a teacher, a neighbor, or someone sitting next to you in school. This will help a lot while you are trying to get through another day and another boring class and some horrible assignment.

Another thing I like about Thomas Edison is that he had no concept of time. He would get involved in his work, pushing an idea forward, and have no idea of how much time had passed, or what day it was, or where he was supposed to be.

As I mentioned earlier, his mother called him "Little Al," which must have referred to his middle name of Alva. So I guess that means Albert Einstein is "Big Al."

> "No man has the right to dictate what other men should perceive, create or produce, but all should be encouraged to reveal themselves, their perceptions and emotions, and to build confidence in the creative spirit."
> —Ansel Adams
> (1902-1984)

---

[1] Who says so about these guys? Thomas Edison and Albert Einstein are described in the book *Driven to Distraction*, by Edward M. Hallowell, M.D., and John J. Ratey, M.D., who are both AD/HD experts. John F. Kennedy and Winston Churchill are identified as having AD/HD in the book *Brainstorms: Understanding and Treating the Emotional Storms of Attention Deficit Hyperactivity Disorder from Childhood through Adulthood* by Joseph H. Horacek, M.D., another AD/HD expert. Horacek also talks about Claude Monet and Amelia Earhart.

Big Al Einstein

Albert Einstein was another early "failure" and late success. When Einstein's dad asked the headmaster of his son's school for advice on guiding Albert Einstein's career, the headmaster of the school answered that it didn't matter, because the kid would never be successful at anything at all.

Ha!

Albert Einstein is the guy who figured out the theory of the universe and ended up getting the Nobel prize in 1921. That pretty much means he was successful—hard to do much better than that. In fact, his name has become synonymous with genius, as in "She's an Einstein...."

Researchers think it's likely that Big Al Einstein had AD/HD. Makes sense to me, not that I'm an Einstein or anything.

Claude Monet

"There are only two things I have ever done well: paint and fidget!" Monet once said.

Claude Monet was a French Impressionist painter, who lived from 1840-1926. He painted a lot of wonderful paintings. They are so famous that you know them, even if you don't know he painted them. Among his most famous paintings are *Water Lilies* and *Haystacks*.

Maybe what he said about himself sums up what all of us with AD/HD have to do. Our job is to fill in this blank. "There are only two things I have ever done well: _____ and fidget!" I need to think that I can do something as well as I fidget or daydream. I have to keep looking until I find something I love to do.

> "Doodling is the brooding of the mind."
> —Saul Steinberg

JFK: John F. Kennedy

John F. Kennedy was president (1961-1963), hyperactive, and so fidgety that one time, in the middle of a meeting at the White House, he fidgeted until the chair he was sitting in busted into pieces. Right in the middle of the meeting.

JFK was also a hero in World War II. He saved his crew after the Navy boat he was in charge of got shot and sank in shark-infested enemy waters. It wasn't JFK's fault that his boat sank, but it was his fault that nobody was going to rescue them. See, he and his boat and his crew took off to fight the bad guys, except that he forgot to tell the Navy where he was going—he forgot to file his battle plans and map. Oops. So when the boat sank, the Navy didn't know where to go to find the crew. JFK didn't let anyone sit around—instead, he got them OUT of there and to safety. And the best thing of all is that, when some kid asked JFK how he became a war hero, JFK said, "It was involuntary. They sank my boat."

Another thing I like about JFK is that he couldn't tolerate heavy clothing or tags in his clothes. One name for this is hypersensitivity (another name for it is tactile defensiveness). This describes people who are extra-sensitive to light pressure put on their skin by, for example, clothes, sock seams, and bed covers.[2] (Some people think that this kind of hypersensitivity is common in people with AD/HD.)

Also, while Kennedy was president, his doctor gave him stimulants that helped him focus and calm down. Staying focused and calm are especially important when you are president, I figure.

> "Human salvation lies in the hands of the creatively maladjusted."
> —Martin Luther King, Jr.
> (1929-1968)

Amelia Earhart

Amelia Earhart was her own kind of wild child, before anybody thought about what you and I call AD/HD. She loved excitement and activity, and dreaded boredom

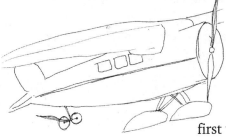

more than just about anything. But she never had many friends. "The girl in brown who walks alone," is inscribed under her picture in her school yearbook.

A lot of people then thought that women couldn't fly airplanes. But Amelia loved airplanes, and in 1935, became the first person to fly the Pacific Ocean from Hawaii to California. She was also the first woman to fly solo across the Atlantic Ocean, and set a ton of speed and altitude records for women pilots.

Helen: You could say that Amelia adored ADDventure!
Bo: You could. But I wouldn't.
Helen: Yeah, that was a cheap shot, but I couldn't resist!

Where Are the Rest of the Women?

This is enough to turn me into a guerilla feminist. The only deceased woman I can find with AD/HD is Amelia Earhart. I know that history has paid more atten-

---

[2] When I was little, I would cut out tags, then the place where I cut them out would drive me nuts. Maybe this has to do with being unable to filter sensory data and pick what you focus on.

tion to dead white males than any women, white or of color.... Grrr. Go make some history, okay?

So What if Some Famous People Had AD/HD?

So people succeed in spite of their AD/HD. Or maybe even because of it. What does that do for you right now? Not much, I admit it.

Still, it's something to think about. If these people managed to handle early failure, then get on to the good stuff, then so can you and I. I hope. It is hard to have AD/HD in this world of organized humans.

On the other hand, there is a lot more support and help for people with AD/HD now than at any time earlier. So maybe things are getting better for all of us, especially us girls with AD/HD.

I keep thinking, though, that if I can find something I love to do—find something to fill in the Monet quote blank (remember?)—"I only do two things well: _____ and fidget")—then I'll do okay. I just have to keep trying to find something I love to do, something that absorbs my attention. At some point, I might see if the guidance office has one of those interest surveys—a kind of test kids can take to help us get an idea of careers that might fit our interests. Even if the test confirms something I already knew, it would still be entertaining to take a test about me instead of a test I have to study for.

"There is nothing permanent except change."
—Heraclitus (450 B.C.)

The Back Page

...

Cheat Sheet

Mostly when you hear about AD/HD, you hear about its adverse effects. But really and truly, having AD/HD is not the end of the world, or even the end of your chances to be anything you want to be. Some of the most successful, famous people have had AD/HD, and in fact, at least for everybody in this chapter, the person's success was at least in part thanks to their own kind of AD/HD!

...

Ask Ms. ADDvice Lady

Dear Ms. ADDvice Lady:

I play in a band, and I think my music is way better when I'm not on my meds. Why should I take them?

Musing about Meds

Dear Musing,

You need to listen to both your muse and your body. But you also need to listen to your family and friends, and maybe your teachers.

Ask them if your music is better when you don't take meds. You might also want to check how you do in school when you are on your meds, compared to how you are when you are off your meds. Also, check with your doctor about your meds.

You'll need to work this out for yourself.

You might choose to take your meds some of the time and not others. For example, if you know that you can pass school when you take your meds, you might want to take them for school. And if you are playing music at night, you might want to use shorter-acting meds during the day, so that you can play the music the way you wish to at night.

But be careful with this. This is a joint effort between you, your doctor, your family, and your muse.

Ms. ADDvice Lady

Dear Ms. ADDvice Lady:

I keep hearing that everybody is special in some way. Well, I'm not. I'm just not. I'm average at everything. It's as if I exist just so other people can look smarter, more athletic, more creative, and more interesting in comparison to me. Oh yeah, and more organized and attentive. Is it OK to just be average?

Batting Average

Dear Batting Average,

Yes. Yes, it is certainly okay to be average. Most of us are average most of the time, or no one would have come up with the word average.

But remember, average is comparative—compared to you, I'm bad at this, and compared to him, I'm good at that.

Comparing yourself to other people has limited value.

The most important thing is NOT how good you are at doing one thing *compared* to somebody else. The most important thing is how much YOU like doing the one thing.

Being "good" at something is really not the point. The point is the pleasure we take in doing it.

For example, I am fabulous at giving advice. This is not something that was apparent in school, in that I have never seen a lesson plan on "advice."

I got average grades. I did average to below average in gym. I did average to above average in reading. I couldn't sew or paint. I rode a bike okay and I could carry a tune. I had some friends.

As far as I'm concerned, that is pretty much, well, average.

And now, I am an advice columnist, and you can see that, in spite of being mostly average while I was in school, I have found something I enjoy doing. I might even be good at it, but the main thing is that I like doing this kind of work.

So somewhere, somehow, if you can hold on, you will find out what you really enjoy doing, and then even if you are average at it, it will make you happy, and so you will no longer be average. Whether you know it or not.

Ms. ADDvice Lady

•••

Fun Facts to Forget

Mozart is another famous guy who (likely) had AD/HD, and the funny thing is that his music is highly structured. Unlike his life....

•••

Chapter 9

Family

As I've said before, AD/HD is just more. More feelings, more distractions, more focus, more problems, more fun, more ideas, more of a pain in the neck, way more frustration. More. That has to do with family, too. Everything is a bigger deal for me than it is for my siblings. It's just MORE.

More is hard to handle, for me, for my parents, for my siblings, even for my aunts and uncles and cousins. Your family may be some combination of step-family, guardian, single parent, grandparent, or whatever, but it's still family, and with AD/HD, it's still a lot to deal with.

Breaking Things

Most of my family problems seem to have to do with breaking things. Like breaking rules. Breaking curfew. And even breaking things. So that's how this chapter is arranged. Each section lists broken things or behaviors that may be common to those of us with AD/HD, along with the AD/HD symptom contributing to the broken thing, and things we can do about the broken thing.

This isn't a comprehensive description of every single family problem that girls with AD/HD can have, but maybe it talks about at least some problems you might deal with. If your family has lots of problems that aren't covered here, your family might want to look into getting family counseling.

Also, just because I list the contributing symptom along with the problem situation, you are NOT off the hook for the results of your actions. Even so, it helps to know how the AD/HD plays into behavior, and maybe why sometimes it can seem like you get into trouble more than other people do. Because maybe we do?

General Methods of Handling Broken Things

To start, here are some general approaches to dealing with problems relating to brokenness.

1. This is the Rule of the Obvious: Don't. Try hard not to make these mistakes. By being aware of them, you have some chance of remembering them. I hope.

2. Once the rule is broken (or whatever is broken), identify the AD/HD reason, at least to yourself and maybe to your parent or whoever is upset with you. This is part of getting to understand why you do the things you do. Self-knowledge. One part of learning to deal with AD/HD is figuring out how it affects you.

3. Cool off, if you need to. I set up a signal so that when I am really angry, I can get off by myself for a bit so that I can cool off. I can't talk if I'm angry that everybody's angry. If you don't have a signal, make one up now and talk to your family about it, so they will give you a chance to get over the emotional reaction and THEN deal with whatever happened, but without the excess anger and frustration or whatever emotion you feel.

4. If you are at all sorry, make yourself apologize. This can be tricky, because I think you have to stick with the truth. Usually I am sorry that I made the mistake or broke the rule or forgot something. But even if I feel like I did nothing wrong, I usually do NOT want to upset people. Usually that means I can truly apologize for upsetting the person who is upset.

5. Talk. Talk to whoever is upset with you. (Again, I usually have to cool down first, because I hate getting yelled at.) Try to understand each other's point of view. If you did something on purpose that is bad, you have to deal with that. But if it is an AD/HD "Oh I Forgot" thing, then you have to try to get that across, too.

6. The next part of talking is to figure out a strategy to help you deal better with the same situation the next time. Sometimes that might include a potential consequence. (Have you noticed that consequence is a code word for punishment?) The consequence might be different if the problem is related to AD/HD. Which reminds me, don't blame straight-up bad behavior on AD/HD— telling the truth is the only way to go. Honest. Then if you do get in trouble due to AD/HD, and you tell the truth about that, your record of honesty helps your parents trust you. Back to strategy. Strategy can include medication change and counseling, if you want to remind your parents of that option.

The Consequence of Consequences Is Sometimes Non-sequential

Turns out that for a lot of kids with AD/HD, punishment doesn't work like it does with other kids. Researchers think that's because of the underlying biochemical differences in AD/HD. Our thinking, or impulsive not-thinking, skips past the prefrontal cortex where the planning and thinking through happens, so we don't take into account the short- or long-term effects of our actions like kids without AD/HD do.

But because standard punishment doesn't work so well, it makes sense to work out a deal between you and your parents, with the help of your counselor. And it also helps to remind your parents that some of your behavior is not malicious. You are not trying to be bad!

Even so, there are going to be results from our actions. It's just that ramping up from "You're late—you're grounded," to "You're late—you're grounded for life" usually doesn't work for girls with AD/HD. So if you are tired of being grounded for life, then you and your parents might want to work out some strategies so you might actually get something out of the process.

Breaking Rules

(These tips below and on the next page can help girls without AD/HD, too!)

What Happens (the rule gets broken)	Contributing AD/HD Symptom	Oops Tip
You come in late, past curfew.	No sense of time.	When you realize it's late, call home right away. Even if you get yelled at, the better late[1] than never philosophy is a good bet. And you might want to work out a system, like your parents will call you or call your friends to find out where you are, in case you forgot.
You mouth off to parents.	Impulsivity, emotionality.	Get away from the situation until you can cool off—maybe signal that you need a break from the problem.
You can't make yourself do a chore or homework.	Low tolerance of frustration, excess emotionality, lack of focus.	This one is hard. You might want to make a plan, like break a big project into smaller bits. Reward yourself when you finish each of the smaller tasks. Maybe you can talk to a friend while you are doing a task, but make sure it's a task that you can do while you talk!

---

[1] Better late than never is a joke about coming in late....

You do something without asking permission.	Impulsivity	The minute you realize you should have asked first, ask or call or try to find an adult to tell. Explain the situation. Be as honest as you can be, as soon as you can.
You forget homework or chores.	Distractible, forgetful, no time sense, problems planning and organizing	Sometimes you just forget. Apologize, talk about it, and next time, get to it the instant you think of it (if you can). And then, create a plan for trying to remember chores and homework, then put it into action. Tell your parents about the plan, too, so they know you're trying.
You don't want to go to family events, or miss them because you forget them (maybe because you don't want to go).	Forgetting or maybe low frustration tolerance and independence kicking in, or hyperactivity keeping you from being able to sit still, depending on the family event.	Another hard one. You might need to work out a deal with your parents on this one. Maybe you could go sometimes when it means a lot to your parents, and skip some that don't matter as much.
You miss appointments.	Poor sense of time, forgetfulness, poor planning and organizational skills.	Need a strategy. Work with parents and friends to help remind you. Maybe try a planner, or a day-timer organizer.
You can't (or won't?) go to sleep on time and then you can't get up on time.	Sleep problems, distractibility (mind keeps going), time sense, executive planning problems.	Exercise earlier in the day can help me get tired enough to actually fall asleep. And to wake up, I put alarms all over my room. Sometimes I sleep through them anyway. Try to come up with strategies for this one.
You lose things, such as cell phones, coats, homework, calculator, socks.	Distractibility, lack of planning, forgetfulness.	One, you need to try to find what you lost, in spite of the frustration. Two, ask friends to help you remember where you put your things. Three, make sure you know where the "lost and found" is in any building you walk into. You get the idea.
You sometimes ruin or break things.	Distractibility, lack of planning, forgetfulness.	It sounds easy to someone who does NOT have AD/HD, but it's hard: don't even pick up someone else's stuff if it's breakable. Look around a room before you leave to make sure you have cleaned up any messes you may have made. Also, when you are handling something fragile, PAY EXTRA ATTENTION. (Yeah, yeah, easy to say, hard to do.)

Getting Along with Parents or Parent-like Units

Everybody's got parent-like units (guardian, foster mother, two mothers, whatever), and each set is different. Mine are pretty understanding when it comes to making AD/HD-type mistakes, which I do a lot of.

I have some friends with AD/HD whose parents get extremely angry when the friends break, or more likely forget, the rules. Grounded for life, no Internet/e-mail privileges, allowance cut off—those kinds of punishments.

It's hard on my parents that I don't learn from past mistakes the way other people do. Not nearly as hard on them as it is on me…. Sometimes they disagree a lot about what to do to help with the AD/HD. They even fight. I hate that.

I know they worry about me.

They worry because of the kind (too many types), frequency (too often), and size (too big) of conflicts we have. Most of the arguments have to do with breaking rules—including unstated rules that you might not even realize are rules, such as not letting your room look like the town dump.

Conflicts Over School

A lot of us have problems with school—our parents expect us to deal with rules and homework and studying, but we bust their expectations about how we should do at school. It might especially bug your parents that you can't seem to bring home your assignments, get started on your homework when you need to, or plan ahead for long-term projects. Or your parents might really have a hard time dealing with your grades after you spaced out in class and didn't hear the teacher discuss what would be on the test—or maybe you didn't even remember that there was going to be a test, so you didn't study.

AD/HD sure plays a role in problems you have with school, but you have to take responsibility for trying to do better. Chapter 11 has some tips for dealing with school and remembering assignments.

Here are some ideas that can help with school battles on the home front.

◎ **Don't expect your parents to do your work for you.** If, in the past, you've let your mother bail you out at the last minute by researching/writing most of a paper for you, resolve not to let this happen again. Instead, get to work on your own, then the next day talk to your teacher and get an extension or work out some kind of project you could do to help make up for turning your assignment in late.

◎ **Set ground rules with your parents about how/when they can nag you about doing your homework.** For example, if your mother always says something that really gets under your skin when she's trying to get you started on your homework, ask her if she would please just say, "It's seven o'clock" to you instead.

◎ **Think up your own ideas of accommodations that could be added to your IEP or 504 Plan to help you bring your grades up.** For example, if you always end up in the back of the classroom where you can't focus because teachers seat you alphabetically, request that you get seated in the front. And let your parents know when you come up with solutions, so they can see you aren't just letting it slide.

Maddy: I did okay in elementary school, but starting middle school meant starting lousy report cards. Even with all the reading my mom has done about AD/HD, she still has a hard time when I get a bad report card.

Helen: I do fine in school. Okay, so I'm a little obsessive about it. But I made some friends and I call them up when I'm not sure what the homework is. It runs my life, though, trying to keep up with everything, so I do get a little wound up about homework. It's either that or I don't do any homework.

Bo: I haven't gotten very good grades since I started middle school. My mom gets upset if I get bad grades because I didn't get my homework done, or because I didn't read the test questions carefully, something like that. So her bad feelings smack into my own bad feelings, then they all bounce around inside of me, then I magnify it all a whole lot more. Then I feel really bad about myself.

Maddy: My dad is more relaxed about my grades than my mom is, but then, he has AD/HD like me, and my mom doesn't. He got bad grades, too, and thinks that I will find some way to cope. But like I said, they do disagree about a lot of stuff, and part of what they disagree about is how to deal with my AD/HD.

Conflicts Over Your Room and Your Chores

I don't care about my room, and I can't figure out why anybody else does. And it isn't that funny when my mom tells me it's because my room is a fire hazard, or that she's afraid of some kind of infestation. Well, I do eat in there and maybe there are some crumbs and some trash.... Anyway, it's *my* room, and who cares what it looks like?

Apparently that is one thing parents have in common. Every single friend with AD/HD I know has to get nagged at to keep her room organized and clean, at least some of the time. My mom isn't a total nag about it, but it gets old, hearing about it.

Helen: My mom is a professional nag about it. We have had some major fights over it. It's a little easier to keep up with the room now that I take the stimulants again. When I wasn't taking any, it was hopeless. I couldn't get started, and if I did, my mom would yell at me about the room after I'd been working on it, and only then would I realize I had spent two hours getting the top of my desk organized and clean, but hadn't even noticed the clothes on the floor or the slop on the top of my dresser or....

Here are some ideas that can help with room battles on the home front.
- Talk to your parents about what specific things really drive them nuts about your room.
- Identify the top big-deal worries your parents have, ones that involve health and safety. Maybe they don't want food and beverages in your room, because of bugs or mold. Or maybe they think matches plus spacey AD/HD is a bad mix, so no lit candles in your room.
- Maybe find out what else annoys your parents, such as the top two things you should keep up with. It helps to know why these things bug your parents, too, at least, if they can explain it. You can't always explain why something bugs you, and that can be true of your parents, too. Maybe your mom hates your clothes spread out on the floor. (The why might have to do with laundry?) Then maybe you can ask to have your own personal dirty clothes basket in your room, or agree that if you don't put your dirty clothes in the hamper, you will wash them yourself.
- Ask a coach to consult with you about organizing your room, or at least get one of your more organized friends to help you come up with some ideas.

Then there are chores. I really do try, but I forget a lot of the time, or after I start, I get distracted. My sister: Miss Perfect. She always remembers her chores, then she brags that her chores are done, and gloats that I'm going to get into trouble.
These ideas might help reduce conflicts over chores:
- Find a time of day when it makes sense for you to do that chore, and try to stick to it. (Brushing your teeth—that works. You just do that every night, don't you?) So, for example, if you're supposed to take the recycling out to the garage every day, get in the habit of

taking out all the recycling, including the cans, bottles, etc. used for dinner preparation, every evening right after dinner.

◎ Think of a way to make it worth it—an incentive. For example, maybe after you clean the bathroom sink, then you get your allowance. Your parents agree not to nag you to clean the sink, but if you don't, you also don't get your allowance. At some point, you'll need money and remember to clean the sink!

◎ Reward yourself for doing your chores. For instance, make a deal with yourself that you can't call your friends until you load the dishwasher.

> Maddy: Don't tell my family, but I do know that some of this mess is my own fault. Oh. I guess if they read this book, they'll know I know. They probably know that anyway. But I do hate doing work, and I do hate chores, and I do hate homework. Who doesn't? I'm pretty normal in the teenager way, I think. My counselor helped me see that some of the reason it's so hard is the added, AD/HD-extra of frustration and emotionality on top of normal teenager I-don't-want-to. I know that it's my problem and responsibility, but I also know that it is harder for me to do some things than it is for other people. It's not an excuse, but it is an explanation.

Conflicts Over Conflict

Even if your parents love you and want to help, they still may not agree (with you or with each other) about how to help or handle things. If your parents don't understand AD/HD, then that's even harder. For instance, they might lecture or punish you for things you can't really control, or constantly compare you to your more organized brother or sister.

If you have a really awful family life, you need to find someone who can help— a teacher, a coach, a school counselor, a priest or rabbi or someone at your church, if you go, or even a nice neighbor, a friend's mother, or one of your relatives. You should also read and educate yourself about AD/HD.

Assuming your parents want to help you, you could give them this book, even if they gave it to you first! Consider asking your parents if you (or your whole family) could try some counseling.

> Maddy: The bad part about my parents having different attitudes about AD/HD is that because dad has AD/HD and doesn't take any meds, he doesn't think I should, while Mom is convinced that I should. I think I am lucky to get the medicine, and actually I think he should take some. So, that is a big source of tension between my parents, which I can't ignore.

I learned how to deal with the tension better, through talking to my counselor. Yeah, I know I'm taking a vacation from counseling right now, but when I did go to a counselor, we talked a lot about family tension because of me having AD/HD. I understand now that the problem isn't me. It's between them. Although I still hate being any part of that tension.

> Helen: We had a different kind of drug war at our house. I didn't want to take the AD/HD medicine, but my folks wanted me to. So I took them for awhile, but I didn't like them. They made me feel shaky, and I didn't feel like myself. Finally I talked my parents into letting me try for a while without them. I did. Then I hated that, too—it was middle school, and I was having a hard time. So, I decided that I needed medications. I had to try like a zillion combinations and I hated that.
>
> I saw this sign on a tip jar at a bagel shop. It said: "Afraid of change? Then put it in here!" That would be me—I don't like change much.
>
> Anyway, the meds are okay with me now, because it turns out I only need a really low dose.

Who Else in the Family Has AD/HD?

AD/HD is often genetic (that was in Chapter 4). So, lots of us likely have one parent with AD/HD, or an aunt or uncle. This can be helpful—or not. For example, your mom might assume that you should be able to handle your AD/HD right now just as well as she handles hers right now, when really, she may have forgotten how hard it was for her when she was your age. She also might have different symptoms, or the same symptoms but to a different degree than you do. Which means she might not understand your flavor of AD/HD.

Or, say your dad has AD/HD—he might be really good at helping you figure out tricks or strategies to get organized, be on time, if he has his own that work. Or he may be too rushed and disorganized himself to be much help.

If you feel as if your parent's AD/HD is complicating home life too much, try:

◎ Giving your parents this book/chapter to read;

◎ Suggesting that your whole family attend an AD/HD convention together;

◎ The strategies mentioned in the treatment chapter—see if your counselor or coach can help you think of what to do, or see if the family might be game for getting some counseling or coaching.

Maddy: My dad has AD/HD. You would think this would help, having someone around who understands what it's like. The answer to that is: sometimes. See, he thinks he's just fine and he's never used any medication. He thinks I should just find some way to deal with living. He doesn't even think it's a big deal that I used to cry all the time, back before I was treated for depression. He thinks that if he just nagged me enough, I would do better. He also thinks that his mom should have nagged him more.

So any more, I don't talk to him about some of the things about AD/HD that are hard. And I know this creates tension between my parents. Oh, good, I say to myself. I'm not only ruining my life, I'm ruining theirs. Well, not really. I know that I am not ruining their lives.

Am I?

Bo: NO!

Helen: NO!

Maddy: Okay, okay. My mom keeps saying she's going to slip my dad some Ritalin just to see if he focuses better, but she's kidding. They do sometimes talk about him taking some AD/HD medications some of the time, though.

And Dad, well, he runs his own business. It turns out a lot of people with AD/HD make excellent entrepreneurs (that is, they start their own businesses). That way, you get to have a lot of ideas and a lot of freedom, and hire other people who can do the stuff you can't. Like keeping the books.

Bo: At my house, it's mom and me. My mom has AD/HD. She has trouble getting organized, too. Because of that, sometimes I'm late or miss out on things completely. It makes me mad. But I forget things too. So it's mostly okay. And mom doesn't bug me about my messy room.

Maddy: I'm glad my mom has done some reading about AD/HD. My dad may have it, but my mom knows more about it than he does! My family is a member of one of the AD/HD organizations. They help keep my mom and me up-to-date on AD/HD news and research.

I know you didn't anticipate that you were anything but an angel and a joy at all times to your family, but from the parent's point of view, children with AD/HD can be a challenge.

Anyway, one researcher, Dr. Judith Kendall, studied families where a child had AD/HD, and pointed out that for the parents, this can be a challenge. One reason is that this is probably not how they pictured life would be when they thought about marriage and having kids. (For example, they probably did not imagine a life that involved raising children in a palace in Beijing or in a fishing village off the coast of Chile, for example.)

So, now these parents have a dreamy or wild-child daughter whose AD/HD makes for some unexpected features of family life. This may be hard for the parents to deal with, since they hadn't planned in that direction. Dr. Kendall's research shows that the best thing the parents can do is work together to accept the idea that their daughter has AD/HD, then set up a new idea of what to expect, or at least give up their maybe unconscious expectations and ideas of what's next. That means that the parents need to lay off any notion that things are going according to some plan. By accepting the AD/HD differences, the entire family can stop spending time being frustrated and start looking forward to what's ahead. It might be especially useful for the father-type person, since studies show that dads dislike treating their kids for AD/HD.

Now that I think about it, this is probably good advice for every parent to deal with every child, since we are all different. And maybe especially good advice for parents lucky enough to have a daughter with AD/HD. You might want to point this section out to your parents, if you think it might help. But also, you might want them to read the good-stuff chapter, to remind them of the good sides of AD/HD. I figure that the odds are pretty good that your parents love you, whether you have AD/HD or not. And anything you can do to understand the world according to your parents' view can help you manage your life with its AD/HD spice. Maybe this section can help them *and* you.

Getting Along with Siblings and Other Family Members

As if it's not enough that AD/HD can break your parents' expectations, it can also sometimes gum up family dynamics in general. This isn't your fault. Everybody's personality and genetic material affect how the family gets along. It's just that the girl with AD/HD may have a more obvious effect on how the family gets along. What I'm talking about, of course, is brothers and sisters and you.

Of course, most brothers and sisters have the occasional (or more than occasional) problem in getting along. There are whole books written on just helping ordinary, everyday siblings get along! Add AD/HD to that mix, and you can end up with problems like:

⊚ Your brother or sister resenting the extra attention or assistance your parents give you;

⊚ You resenting your brother or sister for having an easier time with schoolwork, making friends, or whatever;

⊚ Your sibling thinking you're insensitive because you didn't pick up on some nonverbal cue she thinks she gave you;

⊚ You thinking your sibling is insensitive because she rolls her eyes and sighs when you have to ask her to repeat what she just said;

⊚ Your sibling getting mad at you for losing or breaking her stuff.

So, the problems go both ways. Sometimes I think it would be great if my sister could do a mind-meld with me, so she could understand what my life is like. But I can't figure out how to share brains with her, so instead, I'm trying a bunch of things. You can try them too:

⊚ Help educate a sibling about AD/HD. For example, give her this book to read. Make sure she understands that AD/HD is real and it's not just that you are a slacker who needs self-discipline.

⊚ If you see a counselor, see if your brother or sister can go to that counselor to talk about AD/HD and the challenges of living with a sister with AD/HD.

⊚ Talk to each other when neither of you is upset. Use "I" statements, which are less accusatory-sounding than "you" statements. For instance, say, "I feel really embarrassed when you rag on me in front of your friends about losing stuff" instead of, "You are so mean to bring that up...."

Maddy: Sisters. Another problem. I don't know about brothers. I don't have any. But my older, well-organized sister really doesn't handle the chaos that seems to follow me around and swallow me up. My sister is always complaining because the computer keyboard is sticky (so wipe it off) and my stuff is on the table (I'll get to it). The other problem my sister has is that I am funnier and more talkative than she is, and so I get more attention about that, too. Drives her bananas.

When we are apart enough, it gets easier to be together. We don't go to the same school, and that helps a lot, because she can't act like I embarrass her.

She hardly ever forgets or loses things and then she brags about it, which makes me feel like a loser. (Well, technically, I am a loser because I do lose things.) It's not like I do that on purpose. I figure I'll just have to get a job so I make enough money to replace stuff I lose. And pretty soon high-tech credit cards will need retinal scans or fingerprints or something, so I won't have to worry about losing those. I figure if I do get a cell phone, I'll just put velcro on it, then onto my clothing, so that it sticks to me. Otherwise, it will get lost for sure.

The other thing is that my sister thinks it is unfair that I get all the attention. My response is, who wants that kind of attention? Nagging to get homework done, or worse, friendly reminders, or even worse, having Mom sit down with me when I just can't make myself do my homework. Anyway, it may not be fair that I get some extra attention, but it also isn't fair that I cannot get organized and have inadequate neurotransmitters and that my grade point average reflects the old name AD/HD used to have, which is ADD: A-D-D. My grades.

How come everything is so easy for my sister? I know, it's not all easy, but some stuff, like remembering homework and when tests are and being able to make yourself study prior to the dead last minute—she can do all that. I just can't. Talk about unfair.

Helen: Then we have my littlest brother. I still have to hear the stories about how I used to kick down his tower of blocks and steal the toy he was using. But we have also had some good times—I really understand him, when I have the patience. And now that he's older, we do better, except that I think he resents the attention that his older brother (he has AD/HD) and me get. But he also seems to understand in some way that my parents don't, that I'm trying, hard, and messing up anyway. So mostly, I get along okay with my littlest brother. My other (younger) brother has AD/HD too. Even though we fight a lot, we also get along pretty well the rest of the time, if only because we are always fighting the same battles of trying to get organized and getting yelled at because our rooms are messes.

You may also have to deal with relatives and family friends who inflict good advice on you or your parents, sometimes in your earshot. Especially bad are the ones who don't take AD/HD seriously. Have your parents hand them this book. Brainwashing might also work, but I just can't recommend that!

Get the Family on Your Side

Maddy: I have done some reading (like you are reading this swell book!) and it's helped me understand AD/HD, so I have gotten my mom to read some stuff, too, which helped explain things about me that I can't explain by myself. Also, during my checkups, my mom asks questions about AD/HD.

I might even give this book to my sister, since I know she doesn't really understand the AD/HD thing. It can feel like it's easier to say "you're lazy" or "you're stupid" than it is to understand. I have also been thinking about asking my mom to give a book like this one to my grandma and my aunt and uncle, who seem baffled by, well, me. Understanding what's going on is important. It helped me, so it might help them.

Sometime we might even try family counseling, too, my mom said.

That would be interesting.

Breaking Bones, Laws, Things, and The Bank

These are even more serious issues.

For example, take the issue of driving. Driving statistics for kids with AD/HD are a little scary:

◎ 3 to 4 times more likely to get a speeding ticket than teenagers who drive but don't have AD/HD;

◎ Ditto for accidents;

◎ Twice as likely to lose driving privileges (as opposed to misplacing your license, its own expensive, time-consuming problem).

Obviously, driving and other big serious issues like this can mess up your life—not to mention add to conflicts with your parents. The best way to handle these problems is to prevent them in the first place!

Maddy: I'm putting driving off for another year. My friend, who is mostly attention deprived, already lost her license. I think if I wait, I will have better luck driving. The attention deficit part is a problem with driving. The statistics are bad for those of us with AD/HD, both with money and with driving. So we need to be careful we don't end up some highway mortality statistic. But the statistics are less bad for drivers with AD/HD who TAKE THEIR MEDS. (Hint to any boys who might chance on this paragraph.)

Helen: I like driving. It's also a benefit to my social life, since I can get myself around. I have had a few problems: dented my fender on a raised curb thing at the mall and banged my door into a light pole when I parked too close. But I'm pretty careful, and I really like the freedom of driving. My parents don't let me drive with anyone else in the car, which is not so cool, but it does make sense.

What Happens	Contributing AD/HD Symptom	Oops Tip
Taking some kind of physical risk.	Impulsivity, maybe you like excitement; poor planning, and not thinking about possible consequences.	If you are hanging out with friends, get your most sensible friend to tell you when you are acting on a really bad idea. Also, try to pause before you get going on some wild activity, no matter how much fun it sounds like.
Breaking things because you are mad.	Emotionality, impulsivity.	If you punch your fist through walls or throw things when you get mad, you need to find a better way to deal with your anger. Consider changing medications, if you're taking any, and getting some counseling.
Substance abuse.	Impulsivity, emotionality.	Don't. Instead, think about going for AD/HD medications, if you aren't on any. They work better at what you need help with, anyway.

Taking some kind of legal risk, like thinking the street sign with your name on it needs to be hanging on your wall at home.	Impulsivity.	Don't. You have to practice thinking before you do something like this. Breaking the law is a really, really bad idea. Again, ask one of your sensible friends about any sudden stroke of brilliance you have that might involve you in something you shouldn't be involved in.
Driving too fast, running stop signs, or not driving carefully and getting into an accident.	Distractibility, impulsivity.	Stay off the cell phone and don't eat while you are driving. These things are distracting. Also, don't drive with friends in the car. Accident rates go way up the more kids in a car with a teenage driver, especially an AD/HD driver. One trick here is to delay starting to drive by a year or two.
Spending too much money or even getting into debt.	Impulsivity, low tolerance of frustration (when you want something and can't get it, it can be frustrating).	Don't get a credit card. Don't borrow off your friends. Don't! You need to learn to understand impulse spending and what makes you do it. You also need to think about consequences of getting stuff, and think about the stuff you already have that you can't keep track of.

Maddy: Money's easy: I don't have any. Well, there may be some in my room, under some of the piles. I try not to talk about money to my folks, because boy, does my mom get worried about that one. She is a pretty good sport, most of the time, except when I told her I lost that twenty. Still, she mostly laughs, and now, whenever she supplies me with allowance, she tucks it into something I'm wearing that has a zipper or a snap, like coat pockets.

And my bus pass: I use it to get to school. The current system is working okay. I laminated it, using clear packing tape, and attached it with a long shoelace that is knotted to my backpack. If you laminate money, it doesn't work so well, so I am still fishing for a good system with money things. So, to sum it up, I am bad with sums of money. I can tell this will be a big deal when I go to college.

Helen: I don't have money problems. That same obsessive compulsive thing that helps me get my homework done also helps me track my money. Still, I do have to think about where I put money when I pack it with me—bag? pocket? someplace else weird, like socks?

The Back Page
• • •

Cheat Sheet

It's probably not always smooth sailing with the family, depending on your version of family. Remember that you may make a lot more mistakes than others in your family. Keep trying to deal with AD/HD symptoms before family problems crop up, and deal with the problems directly as you can when they happen. It helps to keep reading and learning, having someone to talk to (like a counselor), reminders (maybe a coach or help from your teachers), and books you can hand around to people like siblings and parents. Also, try to keep lists, write reminders on sticky notes, or notes on your arm, something—always come up with new ways to do the same old thing, and just don't give up, even when things blow up! You can do something about the problems, even though it will probably take more time and effort than you want it to.

• • •

Ask Ms. ADDvice Lady

Dear Ms. ADDvice Lady:

My sister is mad at me because I get more attention. So now I not only get in trouble at school, but my sister makes my life miserable at home.

How do I get her to leave me alone?

Helen Wheels

Dear Helen:

So, your life is "hell on wheels" (a pun), is it? Well, it sounds like it.

First of all, congratulations for writing to me and for reading this book. That is the first thing you can do to help yourself through hard times—learn to understand AD/HD so you can start to use it to help you, instead of just bring you trouble.

The first step in dealing with school AND home is to make sure you understand AD/HD, then to make sure you try to accept that you have it. Once you have that tucked in your pocket, you can talk to your teachers and your sister. Maybe you could even get your sister to read this book. If your parents are willing, you could work with them to try to explain what AD/HD is, and why you get some extra attention. Family counseling helps, too. I would definitely talk to a counselor or someone you trust about ways to deal with your specific situation. You can give your sister information, but you can't change her opinions all by yourself. Work with your family and your counselor.

Ms. ADDvice Lady

• • •

Fun Facts to Forget

Parental statistics: You aren't alone. Genetics is the strongest determiner for AD/HD, which means that the odds are, that if you have AD/HD, one of your parents is 24 times more likely to have AD/HD than are the parents of non-AD/HD kids.

• • •

Chapter 10

Friendship, Love, and a Little about Sex

Some girls with AD/HD have a lot of friends.

Maddy: I do.

Some girls with AD/HD don't have a lot of friends.

Bo: That would be me.

Helen: Hey! Maddy and I are your friends!

Bo: Yes. But the description was "a lot of friends." I do not have a lot of friends. I have you two, and one kid to eat lunch with at school.

This chapter is probably the most useful for girls without a lot of friends. But even if you have a lot of friends, this chapter can help you understand how AD/HD affects your friendships.

You might sometimes assume that everyone with AD/HD would be one way or the other—all of us have friends, or none of us do. But remember when this book compared AD/HD to pneumonia? AD/HD looks different in different people, even though we all have the same thing.

A Note about the Importance of Friendship

This might seem really, really, REALLY obvious, but some girls may have had such bad luck with friendships that it may feel like more trouble than it's worth.

At least to me, it's worth the trouble. You need friends, too. Why, you ask? Because, I answer, otherwise you will die alone, starving and afraid, because nobody likes you, you have no friends, you can't hold a job, and your life is over.

Okay, so that's a little drastic. But having friends is a good thing. For one thing, having friends is practical. You can help them. They can help you. If you forget things, they can remind you. If they are having a bad day, they can call you up and talk until you both chase the friend's blues away.

One thing to remember is that not everyone is going to like you, and you are not going to like everyone. And if you have a problem with anxiety, you'll need to remind yourself that nobody is thinking about you, or judging you, as much as you might be afraid they are.

Finding a real friend, and being one, is worth the trouble.

Why Do Some Girls (and Boys) with AD/HD Have Trouble Making Friends?

What makes it hard for some girls with AD/HD to make friends?

The answer is pretty simple.

Some of us with AD/HD have a lot of things going on in our heads, and we might miss some social cues that most people pick up on.

If you think about it, you were taught how to read and do math. But no one teaches you how to read social signals and make friends. Kids are supposed to teach themselves that, partly by copying older kids and adults. But the symptoms of AD/HD can keep you from noticing these details, which are, after all, pretty subtle. Thanks to your AD/HD symptoms, you might not have learned to read people and social situations. This means that it can be hard to make friends, because you end up not picking up clues about situations, maybe sticking your foot in your mouth, or missing chances to make friends, or behaving in a way nobody else is, just because you didn't read the situation correctly.

This doesn't mean you will never make friends. It just means that you have to work at it more than some girls do. After all, you learned to read books. So you can also learn to read people and social situations. And now that you know about AD/HD, you can also be aware of your AD/HD symptoms that might get in the way of friendship and you can think about ways to minimize problems due to your AD/HD.

This chapter touches on some things you can do, although there are entire books on this subject, like Michele Novotni's book, *What Does Everybody Else Know That I Don't?* In fact, that is a really good book that you might want to look at.

A Reading Lesson: Social Clues

So, since you (may have) missed learning to read social situations and body language, we'll start with that kind of reading lesson. A short reading lesson. You can spend your life learning how to read situations, since the meaning changes depending on where you are.

For example, imagine someone saying, "What's going on?" in the following situations:

An adult walks in on a rowdy party and says, "What's going on?" Underlying meaning: "You better have a good story or you are in big trouble."

A kid walks up while you are reading a book and says, "What's going on?" Underlying meaning: "Want to hang out and talk?"

Your aunt walks in just after you've gotten in trouble, and says to you, in a soft voice, "What's going on?" Underlying meaning: "Are you okay? I'm worried about you."

Same text. But each one of these has different meanings. One word for this is subtext, which is the meaning behind what's being said.

I've had my share of problems reading subtext. One time I joined a Girl Scout troop. These girls had been in the same troop forever, and I was the new kid. And everything I said or did was wrong, wrong, wrong. I felt like I was in bumper cars and that the other cars and posts were invisible. All I knew was that I had banged into something the wrong way, but I didn't know what I had done or said that was wrong.

Bo: That's one reason I don't talk much. I feel like I miss out on stuff. But I don't know what.

Helen: Hey, me too. Makes me wish I could see little cartoon bubbles over people's heads that explained to me what they were really thinking.

Maddy: Yeah, or maybe text, like the words for people who are hard of hearing, that run along the bottom of the television screen, translating what people are saying, except I want it to translate the subtext.

Have you ever had to write a paper about characters in a story, where you are supposed to figure out the theme and motivation and what the story is really about, not just the plot? Basically, you're writing about the story's subtext—how to put together all the pieces, even the ones that seem to contradict, so that it makes sense.

You also need to do that in real life. So part of what you need to learn is the words that aren't being said. You have to turn into a detective.

Bo: I love Sherlock
Holmes
   Helen: I love Agatha
      Christie novels.
Maddy: I prefer Ency-
clopedia Brown....

What detectives do is pay attention to small things, then put together what they mean. That's what you can learn to do. Watch people's expressions and their body language, listen to their tone of voice, and learn to interpret people's behavior. Pay close attention. (I know, that sounds like a joke, given that you have AD/HD. But really, for me it's like figuring out a puzzle or something interesting like that. A game, almost.)

First, just watch people. That's easy to do if you are interested in people. If you aren't, maybe you could get somebody you trust to talk you through what they see as happening in the social situation you are both in. You can also read some books on this subject, too, then use what you learn to interpret what's really going on.

The best rule of thumb might be to be quiet until you've figured out at least some of the rules. When you start at a new school, for example, there might be halls or lunchroom tables sort of "reserved" for a specific group of people. If you hang out there, you might be uncomfortable and wonder why.

Another thing. Watch what people are saying, then compare that to what their bodies are doing. For example, if somebody says "Great seeing you" but they edge away before you can finish a sentence, the body language is saying something you should pay attention to. Here's another example: somebody is hanging around saying "I really have to get going,'" but doesn't make any effort to leave and keeps hanging around. Over a longer period, watch what people say versus what they do, especially if the two don't match. Then think about what the difference means.

Missing the Clues Can Make You Blue (Blue Clues?)

Part of the reason it's important to pick up on social cues is that people don't get it when you miss the clues. They think you got the clues, but that you are disregarding them on purpose. They try to make sense of what you are doing.

This even has a name: attribution theory[1]. People attribute, or assign, meaning to your actions.

When you pick some of our favorite AD/HD symptoms, like being late, or interrupting, or not being able to sit still, then think about what people attribute to the symptom, you have a better idea of what kinds of problems the symptoms might cause with friendships. More about that in the next few pages. First, here are some things you can do that may help you make friends.

---

[1] Heider, F. (1958). *The Psychology of Interpersonal Relations.* New York: Wiley. And the research since then keeps on building on what Heider said.

How to Make Friends and Influence People

Friendship often starts with conversation.

If you have a hard time keeping conversations going, try some of these tips:

- ◎ **Make eye contact.** Catch the eye of the person you are listening to at least some of the time. Of course, you don't want to stare at her, either. But in between, maybe half or even a little more of the time you're talking, make sure your eyes are looking at the person's face. If you aren't sure how much eye contact is good, then when you are in detective mode and are observing other people, watch how often and long other girls make eye contact when they are talking with their friends. Again, don't stare, but you can observe from a distance.

- ◎ **Lean forward when someone is talking to you, and sit still, even if you have to step on your own feet to keep them from jiggling.** Also, make sure you are not all folded up with your arms across your chest and your legs twined around themselves. That makes you look defensive and like you are afraid and don't want to know the other person. If unwinding makes you tense, remember to breathe once in a while, which helps you relax.

- ◎ **Be aware of the distance you are from the other person[2].** Sometimes people with AD/HD don't know how close to get to someone when they are talking. If you are too close, you can spook people. The right distance depends on culture and geography, so watch what others are doing. In general, in North America and when you are talking with someone you don't know well, stand at least two or three arm-lengths away, assuming circumstances allow. If the person is moving into the friendship category, then one or two arm-lengths is enough. You can get to where you can guess that distance, just by paying attention.

- ◎ **Listen, really listen to people, even if it means ignoring the chatter in your head and all the good ideas and jokes you think of.** One way to be sure you are listening is to sometimes echo back what the person is saying.

- ◎ **Ask people about themselves and clamp your mouth shut so you don't interrupt.** You might want to bring up things that you have in common and that you find interesting and already want to know more about. This helps you pay serious attention to the conversation and the person.

---

[2] There is even a word for personal space—the distance you stand from somebody. The word, *proxemics*, was suggested in 1963 by E.T. Hall, a researcher.

When you are getting to know people, try really hard not to jump to conclusions about anybody.[3] That's important partly because you need people to accept you the way you are, so you should do the same for them.

One Way to Start Making Friends

First, find someone you would like to be friends with, or, if you don't know anybody because you are new at the school or club or whatever, watch for a little bit, and pick someone, or find someone else who doesn't seem to know anyone.

Walk up to the person and stand or sit (whatever that person is doing), about four feet away (unless you are at a basketball game and can sit next to them and it isn't awkward to do that). Then say something, maybe that you've practiced a little before you walk up, but something low-key, like "Good game, don't you think?" or "I hate waiting in line, don't you?" or "How long have you been coming to this club?" It helps if you end in a question.

The next part can be hard for someone with AD/HD. That is, a friend needs to be able to listen. Ask questions. Then listen some more. Concentrate on the other person, not on the fact that you are nervous or feel uncomfortable. Try to bring up a subject the other person is interested in, or better yet, that you both might be interested in. And don't forget humor, which is a big help in pretty much all social situations. So are manners, for that matter. Practice them beforehand, if you aren't very good at them. But saying "hi" and "bye" and "thanks" and "excuse me" all just make social interactions easier.

Bo: I try to think about the other person. I get nervous if I think about myself.

Helen: Hey, I'll have to try that the next time I get nervous talking to somebody.

Bo: My parents asked if I wanted to take a social skills class, but instead, I read a book that helped. That Novotni book.

Helen: Cool. I should read it.

So Maybe She Could be a Friend

If you think somebody might be a friend, try to pace yourself. Don't act too enthusiastic, too fast, because that might scare him or her off.

---

[3] Did you ever read *The Phantom Tollbooth*, by Norman Juster? I can't say Jump to Conclusions without thinking of that book.

Maddy: I do that sometimes. I used to tell myself I didn't mind, I didn't want them as friends. Then I learned to go more slowly, so it doesn't happen that often. And now, if I scare somebody off, it is actually true that I don't want to be their friend. I need someone who can accept even the over-energetic parts of me.

Bo: I have the other problem. I have to make sure the person doesn't mind me being quiet.

Helen: That works great with Maddy, because she talks a lot.

Bo: I'm always grateful when someone is kind of chatty, because it takes the pressure off of me.

Maddy: I'm always grateful when you don't make me feel like I talk too much, even if I do talk a lot.

Helen: Maddy, it's okay! I am glad you have a lot to say. I think you are interesting! And I'm not that quiet, myself, as you have noticed, I'm sure.

Maddy: I think you're interesting! Oh, I get it. That's what you think about me, maybe…. Anyway, when I am getting to know someone, I try to pay attention to how I feel really. Does this person seem like somebody I could be friends with? Or do I just want this person to be friendship material? I also have to try to talk less than usual. It's easy to overload someone with too much information at the beginning, because I'm so chatty. I have to make myself go slowly when I am making friends.

Remember that friendships are balanced, not tilted in either direction all the time. If you have to do all the calling and arranging, or if the other person is always telling you what to do, this isn't balanced. Friendships work best if you feel like you are equals most of the time.

If a potential friend is upset, listen, repeat back, and try to put yourself in her position and imagine what she is feeling. Unless asked, don't try to solve the problem. Most of the time, people want to talk and want empathy more than they want to solve the problem. If the person wants to solve the problem and starts asking you, that's different. But usually it's a good idea to wait until the other person moves into the area of what-do-I-do before you start dumping advice on him or her.

Also, remember that you need to accept that other person the way she or he is, just as she or he needs to accept you the way you are. After all, with AD/HD, people might have to adapt to your style a little bit, what with our forgetfulness and all.

Maddy: With friends, I always try to find a different way to get it wrong.

Helen: Oh, very funny.

Bo: No. Wait. I see. In a way, Maddy makes sense. You learn not to make that exact mistake again. So you're finding a way to make different mistakes....

Maddy: That's what I meant!

Helen: Oooh, now I get it. Yes, that is a good idea.

How Others Interpret AD/HD Symptoms

Here are a few examples of AD/HD symptoms that can lead others to falsely assume things about you, and some ideas about what you can do when you find yourself up against these attributions.

The You're-Late Example

You are supposed to meet with two other kids the teacher assigned you to work with on a group project. You forget about it, and they call you and ask where you are. By the time you show up, you've missed half the work session.

What the other two kids might very well think goes like this: "She didn't come because she's lazy. She's trying to make us do the work."

Although what happened, of course, is you demonstrated your basic AD/HD lack of planning and lack of any sense of time.

In fact, you might have been looking forward to working on this project, depending on the project and the kids.

What Can You Do About This One? Here are a few ideas: warn other kids you are doing assignments with that sometimes you are late or forgetful. Don't bring up AD/HD unless you feel it is okay to do. You might want to ask the friendliest of the group to give you a reminder call. If no one seems friendly and you don't want to go that route, put reminders everywhere, or ask a real friend to remind you, or someone (maybe at home) who is willing to help you keep track of a schedule. Also, you might want to mention to the teacher that you forget things. More on that in the school chapter. If you have a counselor, maybe the counselor can help you come up with solutions.

The You-Interrupted Example

You join a book group discussion club at school, and you are so excited. You show up at the library (pretty close to on time, this time!), and you jump right into the conversation about the book.

One girl was talking when you walked in, and you started talking because what she said was just what you had been thinking.

The interrupted girl, and others in the book group, might think that you are rude and that you think that you are a know-it-all.

Although what really happened, of course, is due to your basic AD/HD impulsivity. Their attribution, that you think you are so smart, is way off base.

What Can You Do About This One? Here are a few ideas: the minute it occurs to you what might have happened, be careful not to interrupt again. If you realize in time, you could say, "Oops, I'm sorry. I got so excited about your idea that I interrupted." Then let others talk. Otherwise, you could go out of your way to ask the interrupted kid's opinion later in the conversation. If you think the person you interrupted looks like the kind of person you could talk to, then after the book club apologize quietly, without making too big a deal out of it, even if it's a big deal to you. Also, if you have a counselor, maybe the counselor can help you come up with things you could do.

The next page shows a list of some AD/HD traits to watch out for and suggestions about how to handle each one.

Good Friendship Traits: Remind Yourself!

Girls with AD/HD have some advantages when it comes to making and keeping friends, along with some disadvantages: a mix. Remember the positive qualities!
- Loyal and honest;
- Because we forget so much, we usually don't tell secrets;
- Funny;
- Unpredictable, so we're always interesting to be around;
- Loving and deeply connected to our friends;
- Compassionate and empathetic;
- Spontaneous: we go along with whatever's going on and have a good time.

Telling Friends You Have AD/HD: Training Your Pals

This is one that you have to figure out for yourself. On this topic, talking to a counselor or some adult or other friend you trust can come in handy, while you try to figure out whether the person you are becoming friends with wants to hear about AD/HD. Every situation is different. Partly, it depends on how you feel. If having people know you have AD/HD doesn't bother you, then it might be easier to talk about it. And certainly it's a good idea to pay attention to your gut feeling about it. Trust your intuition.

Trait	Symptom	Possible Attributions	Some Ideas of What to Do
Hyperactivity	You fidget.	The other person thinks you aren't listening, and that you are thoughtless or self-involved because you don't listen.	You can try to sit still (sit on your hands). You can make more eye contact. If you trust them, tell them you have AD/HD.
No sense of time	You're late.	The other person thinks that you don't care about her or him.	You can warn the person ahead of time that you are forgetful and that you have no sense of time. You can set a timer or something to remind you. You can ask someone you trust to help you remember in time to be on time.
Forgetful	You forget things, like birthdays.	The friend thinks that you don't care about her or him.	Tell the person you have AD/HD. After all, if it's a birthday, they must be a real friend. And give the friend a belated gift or card.
Impulsive, low tolerance of frustration, and you get too emotional	You get into a discussion and you say something that later you wish you hadn't.	The other person can't forgive you for what you said because the person figures you had thought about this a long time and so meant it.	Apologize! Try to explain how AD/HD works. Try to stop the minute you know you crossed the line and tell the person you didn't mean it the way it came out. Hand her this book.
Easily distracted	You lose track of the conversation.	The other person assumes that you find her boring and maybe decides to stay away from you.	Apologize; ask your way back into the conversation. Periodically repeat something the other person is saying in a supportive way, to keep yourself on track. Make eye contact as often as feels right, to help you stay tuned in.
Impulsive	You interrupt.	The other person thinks you are rude and thoughtless and think what you have to say is more important than what she is saying.	Apologize for interrupting. Try hard to wait until everyone finishes speaking. Mention that you find yourself interrupting and wish you didn't.

Maddy: I used to not want to talk about having AD/HD, but after a while, I realized it was hopeless to try to explain myself any other way, so I've become AD/HD Girl. I need a cape and a few superpowers, and I'll be ready to go. Maybe I'll get a tattoo that says AD/HD Girl!

Or not.

Anyway, if I find myself in a situation where I just know AD/HD is going to make for trouble (like working with other kids on a big project), I just tell the other kids that I have AD/HD. And mostly that works okay. It's amazing how people open up when you tell them something like that about yourself. I've learned that lots of people have lots of stuff going on. One of my best friends, Karla, and I together agree that Karla has AD/HD, even though she hasn't been diagnosed. We think Karla also has obsessive compulsive disorder (OCD). Then I tell her I wish I had some of her OCD, and she says fine, you can have it, but she won't take any of my depression, sheesh. Because I am willing to talk about having AD/HD, I've found out a lot about other kids in my classes. One of my friends is a superb artist and she has bipolar disorder. And a lot of the girls I know have either taken antidepressants or talked to a counselor at some time or other.

Sometimes, it is clear that the person I'm talking to thinks I'm faking it or that AD/HD isn't real or something equally supportive (NOT). So I just change the subject. If the person keeps bugging me about it, I tell the truth—that it doesn't do any good to talk to somebody about something when they won't listen. Because usually they just want to argue and say it isn't real or that I'm just lazy or whatever.

Eventually, I shrug my shoulders and walk away. I've learned that I don't have to take any abuse from anybody about it.

Like I said, most people start talking to you about their lives if you start talking openly about yours. It helps if you are matter-of-fact, I think because it makes it easy for the other person to be nonjudgmental and matter-of-fact. People are some-times afraid of emotions, even though I think that is silly. Anyway, I have found that if I stay calm and just bring AD/HD up without making a big deal, people seem okay with it most of the time. I also make jokes—most people appreciate a sense of humor, especially when you gently poke fun at yourself. They see that you aren't taking yourself that seriously, even if you have brought up a serious topic like AD/HD.

My favorite AD/HD joke is this one, that I made up:

Question: How many AD/HDers does it take to change a light bulb?

Answer: Want to go for a bike ride?

Get it? Zero attention span

(CONTINUED . . .)

Bo: I don't talk about AD/HD. It's nobody's business. Once I get to know someone and trust them, I might talk about it. Until then, forget it. I don't say anything.

I'm not matter-of-fact, though. I go home and sweat and worry about what I said. Sometimes the person I'm talking to acts like she doesn't want to hear it. Even worse, she might act like AD/HD is fake. So I clam up. Which is easy.

Helen: Me? I don't care. I'll talk about it. Or not. Depends on if it comes up. I talk a lot, so it just dribbles out of my mouth.

Bo: I wish. I think it's plain hard. Sometimes I feel like I walk around labeled. Other times I forget that I have AD/HD. Then it feels like it's my fault that I mess up. I feel like a failure. Then I might remember I have AD/HD. Even so, it feels like a lame excuse.

Helen: You should hang around me, then! I'll remind you, at least when I remember, and I'll talk about it so you don't have to.

Bo: Actually, that sounds great!

Friendship and Gender

One characteristic of AD/HD is that we can act younger than we are—at least, that's what researchers find. I see this as a good thing, because that means we have more time to watch and catch up on general social skills, and we get along well with younger kids, too. I don't mind letting other kids venture into dating before me. That lets me see what is coming, and what it is like from my friend's point of view.

Helen: Are you kidding? I don't want to be socially behind!

Maddy: Well, I decided I don't care, and in fact, I think it's good that we aren't necessarily boy crazy at an early age. In fact, for awhile in middle school, I wondered if I was gay, because so many other girls were boy-crazy and I just wasn't. I thought about it, and realized I wasn't romantically interested in either boys or girls. It helped when I got diagnosed with AD/HD and read about how we might be a little behind, socially.

Bo: My mom always wants me to be friends with lots of kids, boys and girls.

Helen: I think boys are easier to be friends with. You two excepted, of course! But you don't mind about the socially behind thing?

Maddy: I just don't. I think friendship can be hard, whether you have a lot of friends or only a few friends. So waiting on romance sounds good to me.

Dating

When it comes to dating, we girls with AD/HD have a few things we have to be careful about. Very careful.

For one thing, being in love with someone releases dopamine. Yes, we are back to brain stuff. That means that it can be very easy for us to fall in love. It's a kind of self-medication. Also, girls with AD/HD can be very, very intense. What that means is that you can get wonderfully lost when you are in love, in the infatuated-beginning parts of love, especially.

One thing that helps keep things in balance is continuing to take your medication—if you are taking any, that is. That way you aren't at the mercy of the love-induced or infatuation-induced dopamine rush. It will help you stay level, whichever way things go.

Girls with AD/HD (and boys with AD/HD, too) tend to fall in love fast, get furiously involved, but then have short-term relationships. Maybe the relationships are short because we can't keep up that level of intensity for that long. Also, we are distractible and if something new comes along, we might get pulled into it.

Maddy: Dating. Well. Not my area of expertise. I don't have anything personally to say about guys, except that if I like them, I talk too much around them. I get nervous, which makes the AD/HD even worse. Sometimes I babble even when I don't like them. Then I feel like a total fool.

Helen: I think the friendship part of dating is the most important.

Maddy: If you don't like being socially behind and you have an opinion on dating, then why don't you talk about dating?

Helen: Okay. I will.

Helen on Dating

Start with friendship. The main thing you have even when you are dating is friendship. That means someone you can talk to and be yourself around. If you can't be yourself, that's a clue that something's out of whack.

Love is not just a feeling. It is also a friendship with the other person, and a way of caring about the other person that is built on knowing the person. You cannot get to know someone if you are just infatuated like a wild-child. Not that infatuation is bad. You just have to be careful and not let yourself get too intense too fast, or you risk burning out on the relationship.

Remember to listen to your friends and family. If they don't like the person you are seeing, that is a clue that maybe you got swept off your feet too fast or maybe didn't read the person correctly. This goes back to the question of how well you read social cues, which is something a lot of people with AD/HD have trouble with.

If you want a relationship to work for at least a while, be prepared to make some extra efforts. Eventually, in any kind of friendship, the newness wears off, and then the AD/HD distractibility can really get in the way. You'll need to spend time getting to know the person, and also keep track of your other friends and the rest of your life so you don't depend too much on one person. Putting your entire bunch of needs on one relationship puts it under a lot of pressure. Be careful of that if you want to keep being with the person.

If you do have a counselor, you might want to talk about your relationship as it goes along, so that you keep aware of it and can take care of it if things start to drift.

Helen's Dating Clues

1. You likely won't be yourself when you first go out with someone. If you like the boy (or girl) but don't know him well, you are busy trying to figure out who he is, learn more about him and how he feels, and also, you want him to like you. Hard to be at ease in that situation.
2. At some point (not the first ten minutes or even the first few times you hang out) you probably need to bring up the fact that you have AD/HD. It's important to tell the truth to someone who is your friend, or more than that.
3. Take your time. Don't get way too intense way too fast, which can be an AD/HD thing to do.

A Little about Love and Sex

The physical attraction part of a relationship is, uh, very attractive. Very.

So those of us who are high on the impulsivity scale had better be careful. CARE-FUL. For example, when you are fooling around is NOT the time to let the hormones make your decisions. You need to use your brain, some patience, and protection. That means emotional protection, too. In other words, you need to decide BEFORE you find yourself in the throes of passion how far you are willing to go.

I'm not here to lecture. Just don't get pregnant, or AIDs. Both of these are extremely bad scenarios.

So, think before you get into the situation, practice what you're going to say, and when in doubt, wait. Thinking ahead of time, when we are alone and not anywhere near the boyfriend, is especially important because when we are in love, the dopamine can be a real rush. And anyway, we might tend to be very emotional, very impulsive, and very intense. Put that into the dopamine- and hormone-rich mixture of love, and it gets even more important to be careful. If you are really nervous, double-dating might be a plan for those times when you think you are in a more impulsive mode.

If you find that you aren't sure what to do, or if you've gotten yourself into a mess, find an adult or friend you can trust and talk to them.

This is pretty solid advice for non-AD/HD girls, too, by the way.

Love.

Love is kind of the point of the whole thing, anyway. Friendship, relationships, doing what you love—doesn't matter if it's playing the piano or playing with your dog. The love part—the part that sets you free—that's the point of living, at least for me.

Just a friendly reminder....

The Back Page

• • •

Cheat Sheet

Your brain may have been busy doing other things when other kids were learning about social cues. Also, you might be socially a year or two behind. And lastly, some traits that might have to do with AD/HD can interfere with being friends (impulsive, distractible, looks like we aren't paying attention because we can't sit still when we talk to someone, and so on).

AD/HD is just fabulous, isn't it?

Anyway, this combination is a pain in the neck when it comes to making friends. The good news is that you can learn about the social cues you missed out on, you'll catch up socially if you cut yourself some slack, and you can learn about any symptoms you have that might interfere with friendship, then be aware of them.

Also, remind yourself of some of the good things you bring to the friendship that maybe the AD/HD contributed to.

And be very, very, very careful when it comes to romantic involvement.

• • •

Ask Ms. ADDvice Lady

Dear Ms. ADDvice Lady:

My friends tell me I'm "too intense" and I'm afraid that the guy I like will think that too, especially since this chapter talks about AD/HD people being in intense relationships that burn themselves out. What should I do?

Unintentionally Intense

Dear Intense,

Balance. Moderation.

Aren't those difficult?

In any friendship, regardless of your friend's gender and the nature of the relationship, you have some fundamental characteristics that are central to who you are. If you don't like who you are when you are intense, that's one thing—trying to be less intense might be a good idea. But if intensity is something that you value about yourself, then you'll have to tread

carefully so that you don't scare people off *or* try to make
yourself into something you aren't.

The middle ground is there—it just might take you a while
to find it—when to lighten up, when to be intense, when to
ignore the urgency of your feelings, when to pay attention to
them. This is plenty hard for all teenagers, and it can be especially hard for women with AD/HD.

So, don't sacrifice who you are, and at the same time, try to
tone down any tsunami tendencies to overwhelm others. You
can do this!

Miss ADDvice Lady

•••

Fun Facts to Forget

Turkey and tryptophan, dieting and depression. Have you ever gotten
sleepy after a turkey dinner (say, Thanksgiving dinner)? This is sometimes
said to be caused by the tryptophan in turkey. So, that's where you might
have heard of tryptophan.

It turns out that tryptophan is a precursor of serotonin (tryptophan is a
large molecule that gets busted into smaller molecules—in this case, serotonin). Serotonin helps regulate mood. So getting adequate tryptophan can help
keep you from being moody. Tryptophan is found in more foods than turkey.

The moral of the story: if you are dieting, make sure you keep eating
tryptophan-laden foods, which include milk, cheese, bread, and bananas.
This might help you with your serotonin levels, which means, you could be in
a better mood if you eat a banana... and that, if you aren't eating enough
tryptophan, dieting might truly BE depressing.

•••

Chapter 11

School

AD/HD Symptoms Can Be Anti-School

School. Should be a four-letter word. Like AD/HD. Four letters that pack a punch.

Not for everyone, of course. Some girls (and boys) with AD/HD are way organized and also very busy. Maybe because it's constantly interesting if you have a lot to do and it's a game to see if you can keep on top of it. For those kids, school is easier than it is for the daydreamy and disorganized among us.

I, myself, am spectacularly disorganized, if I do say so. My locker tends to look as though a jumbo firecracker just went off.

For those of us for whom school is hard, it can be really hard. And because we spend so much time at school, school gets a lot of pages in a lot of books.

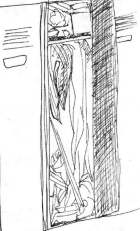

What about AD/HD Makes School Hard, Aside from Everything

Let's review, class. Some AD/HD symptoms, such as distractibility, impulsivity, and day-dreaminess mean that we tend to have an unavoidably hard time with a lot of parts of school.

Thing That Is Hard to Do	AD/HD Symptom That Makes the Thing Hard to Do
Paying attention, focusing on one thing (such as the subject of the class)	Distractibility, day-dreaminess
Being still in class	Hyperactivity
Talking only when called on, not interrupting	Impulsivity
Waiting to be called on, waiting in line, waiting for tests to be handed out. Waiting.	Low tolerance of frustration
Keeping track of time	No time sense
Staying out of social trouble and making friends	Distractibility means that we may not have picked up on social cues when we were little
Being awake	Sleep problems

Did I forget anything? (That's another joke. Since I forget most things.) Oh. I forgot forgetting.

Remembering homework, tests, projects, and so on	Memory, distractibility, day-dreaminess

The Usual Things You Can Do

This section is one of the ones I am including even though you might have heard this a million times before, in which case, scan it and keep going. But if this is pretty new to you, read on.

Helen: *These tips are in every AD/HD book ever written (at least, that's what Maddy and I think). So I know Maddy was reluctant to include them.*

Bo: *On the other hand, we forget things often enough so maybe it doesn't hurt to include it.*

Maddy: *Thank you both. Yes, here are some school survival tips that you can try, and apologies in case you've heard or read this way too many times.*

Planners, and Yes, I Figure You've Heard This Before

Use a planner. Write down your homework assignments. At least, in theory, it's a great idea. Now, for me, if the planner could be reduced to a microchip and attached subdermally, maybe. But instead, it's paper, and I can be guaranteed to forget it. If you know you are likely to forget assignments, make sure you have the email address or phone number of at least one dependable student in each of your classes.

If you have a 504 Plan or IEP (see Chapter 6), use the accommodations in the plan to help make sure your assignments make it home. For instance, there could be a require ment that a teacher or another (non-hostile, of course!) stuc check your assignment book to make sure you've written it down right, or that the teacher write the assignment on the board instead of mumbling it at the end of class, or that you be allowed to keep an extra set of textbooks at home.

> Bo: I use a planner. Sometimes I forget, but when I start using a planner again, it helps. It goes in cycles.

Contracts

Did you ever hear about signing a contract with your parents or the school? Basically, a contract is a written agreement. It sets out the rules, clearly, and in writing. It may also set out what you will "earn" if you follow the rules. Kids (both with AD/HD and without it) use contracts to set out expectations clearly, and to help make sure everybody understands and agrees to the rules. Some kids have contracts for homework, driving, school behavior, lots of things.

If you have not used a contract before and want to try, start small. Don't try to solve all your problems in one fell swoop. Write down the one or two most important things you would like to do better at and pick a reward that's rewarding enough to motivate you to try to change.

Helen: I use one. Maddy, put mine in this chapter. It's a contract I worked out with my parents.

Maddy: Okay. It's at the end, because it's kind of long.

Helen: Cool. It helps me a lot. It would be great if it helped somebody else.

Maddy: I wish contracts worked for me.

Surviving School: Find Things That Work for You

Let teachers and a counselor know you have AD/HD. If you have an IEP or 504 plan, you can write tips like the ones in this section into the plan. If you don't have a plan, work with a counselor or find a few minutes to talk with your teacher early in the semester or before semester classes start. After all, you know your school patterns. So, if you know you are going to daydream or talk in class, you could tell the teachers about your AD/HD and whatever bad habits they can look forward to. Ask for their help in NOT embarrassing you since you can do that all by yourself without their help. For example, ask the teacher to please not call on you if you are in space-mode, and to stand by your desk if you get chatty or need to pay attention. If the teacher doesn't seem to believe you, talk to a counselor, your parents, or another adult to help convince the school to give you a hand.

Part of dealing with AD/HD might be trying a lot of different ways to deal with each problem. Variety helps keep things interesting. And for me, interesting means that there's a better chance I'll stick to it.

You can read through all the tips in the world, but you have to actually give the tips a try to make them work. Pick the tips that sound right to you—that make sense and feel like something you can actually do.

Bo: I think that's why I sometimes use my planner and sometimes I don't.

The chart on the next few pages lists some suggestions that anyone can try or start with as an idea, and it includes the Maddy-specific version of how to handle what's hard.

What's Hard	General Advice	Maddy's Advice
Getting up in the morning.	Get ready for school (lay out your clothes, find lunch money) before you go to bed, so that you don't have to remember quite so much in the morning. Use one, two, or more alarm clocks. Put them far enough away that you have to get out of bed to turn them off. If you have a radio alarm, tune it to a radio station you HATE. If you have two radio alarms, set each one to a different radio station you hate and I bet you fly out of bed in the morning to shut them off in a hurry. Ask a family member to make sure you actually get up.	My latest attempt at getting up in the morning is to make sure that I don't have to do anything except put on clothes, grab something to eat, pick up my backpack, and leave. I shower the night before, dump things on top of my backpack, and pile up everything I need. I have for now given up on an alarm clock. I have trained myself to sleep through them. Instead, I rely on one of my parental-units who has to go to work anyway.
Getting to class on time.	Set your watch a few minutes early. Find someone to help remind you to get moving between classes.	Earlier in the school year I'm better at this than later. Sometimes I find somebody in the class to hook up with, who is on time, to help me remember to get to class on time.

Remembering to take things to school.	Pile everything you might need on or near your backpack.	If I don't put everything in a big pile on my backpack, it is pretty sure not to make it to school.
Not getting into trouble in class when I daydream.	Sit near the front of the class and make eye contact with the teacher. Also, you might want to work out a deal so that when the teacher notices you are drifting, he or she can signal you in a way that is quiet and not embarrassing but that gets you to focus.	I am trying to get to know somebody in every class, so I can get them to poke me if I start daydreaming or talking or finding some other way to ignore a lecture.

Keeping track of homework, projects, papers, tests, presentations, quizzes, then getting them done or studied for.	Try taking a study hall.
	    Try using a planner.
	    Ask friends about assignments.
	    Ask the teacher for an extra copy of assignments and projects, and put the spares on the refrigerator or in your room.
		Friends in class. I need help remembering all this stuff, because otherwise, I just don't remember. I am taking a study hall this semester. It helps. While I'm there, I can work on whatever I inevitably forgot about.
		    I also write things on my hand the minute I realize that I have homework, and also, I wear a lot of clothing with pockets so I can stash important papers if I don't have my backpack right with me.

Getting along with the kids who disapprove of my very existence.	Try to get to know the kids a little, to see if that takes care of it.
	    Talk to your friends about what you might be doing that others see as "weird." Write about it, or talk to a counselor.
		At one school, I felt like I was surrounded by kids who thought I was weird.
		    Usually, if I can spend some time with people, we end up getting along. Otherwise, I end up talking to my counselor about it.

Getting angry and frustrated.	Set up an escape hatch so you can leave the room and go somewhere like the bathroom or the library, so you can cool off and teachers know where you are.	Since I get frustrated in math, I talked to my math teacher and she lets me scribble a note on a piece of paper saying where I'm going (or two places, like the library and the cafeteria, if I'm not sure), then I can slide it on her desk when I make my escape.
Letting friends get you in trouble.	When your resistance is low (like maybe you haven't slept well), hang out with friends who are less likely to get in hot water.	I get in more trouble when I hang out with the other kids with the especially hyperactive version AD/HD. Sometimes I go sit by the daydreamy kids with AD/HD, instead of the chatty ones....

Remembering to bring lunch.	Bring extra some days, so that you don't mind bumming food off friends when you do forget. Stash some energy bars or emergency lunch funds in your locker and backpack for emergency use. Make a no-refrigeration-required lunch the night before and put it into your backpack. (Peanut butter sandwiches are great that way.)	The high school I go to is across from a grocery store, so I can either use money I remember to bring, or bum some off my friends and then have to remember to pay them back, which isn't as hard as it sounds because when I do bring money I bring enough to pay people back, and lunch is every day, so I do remember sometimes. Sometimes I even make my own lunch.
Doing homework.	Routine. Get a friend to study with. Make it a deadline with a reward, like getting it done in time to watch your favorite TV show.	That is so hard, and it seems to be so easy for my sister. Still, if I wait until the pressure builds, or if I stay up late, sometimes I can make myself do it. Once in a while I can even do it at a reasonable hour, but not usually.
Trying to keep track of your things.	Work on making habits that reduce the chaos factors. For example, keep every bit of homework inside your backpack and always zip your backpack. Color might help to keep things together for you. You, and maybe a counselor or a parent, could sort through papers and subjects, and give each one a color. Then when you see green, you'll know it's history, or blue, and you'll know it's biology.	At home, I've got this one spot that my family knows about and where the clutter won't bother everybody any more than it has to. I keep all my school things in one place. Every time my mom or I see a textbook or paper, we deposit it on top of my school pile.
Getting to bed and to sleep.	Get into a routine so you go to bed at a regular time. Make yourself relax by stretching gently, then letting go. Play soft music or turn on a fan to block out household noise.	Now here's another hard one: going to bed. Sometimes I can merge homework, showering, and going to bed in a jumble and get them done, but not usually until pretty late. Then I'm back in trouble getting up in the morning.

Learning Styles

To survive school (and maybe life, but I wouldn't know about that just yet, since school is the hard part for me) it can help to know what your learning style is. Learning style is how you soak up information the best. People sort learning styles into all sorts of types. Here are the ones I found out about that make sense to me:

- Visual (learning best by looking at pictures, reading, watching demonstrations)
- Physical (learning best by actually doing things, or by moving around while you are learning)
- Auditory, or hearing (learning best by listening to lectures, books on tape, etc.)

How do *you* learn? Take the quiz on the next page and circle the answers that best describe you, then you can try out ways of studying that fit each learning style.

Interpreting Your Score

If you have mostly **a**, then you are a visual learner—you see the information in your head, or sometimes even see the letters of the words.

If you have mostly **b**, then you are a physical learner—you like to DO things.

If you have mostly **c**, then you are an auditory learner—you learn best by hearing the information out loud

A lot of people learn well in a couple of ways. If you split pretty evenly, then you can probably adapt to different types of learning. If you are really big on one, you might want to skew your study habits in favor of methods that emphasize that learning style, (which I talk about in the next sections). And no matter what, as an authentic AD/HD girl-child, it can't hurt to have a lot of choices—keeps things from being dull!

If You Are a Visual Learner

When you are talking or listening to someone, think about whether you see words (the letters spelled out) or pictures or both. Some people see words. I do. I definitely have to use language to find out what I think and know, and study using words and diagrams. One of my artist friends is a visual learner, too, but she thinks spatially, which I do NOT. Anyway, whichever kind of visual learner you are, you could try some of these:

- Write and rewrite the material you are trying to learn, so that you see it on the page.
- Write outlines.
- Keep notes on subjects you are studying. If you own the textbook, you can write in it as you read.
- Use flashcards.
- Use highlighters or colored pencils to color code information you are trying to learn.

How Do You Learn?

Question	Answer
1. Which is your favorite class (or at least, least bad class)?	a. History, because you get to write things down. b. Theater or gym, because you get to move around. c. Spanish class, with a lot of talking and listening.
2. What is the least awful kind of homework assignment for you?	a. Research paper or a creative writing assignment. b. Improv or skit. c. Presentation or speech.
3. What is the best (which means least awful) kind of class format?	a. Lecture with diagrams and lots of visual elements. b. Lab work or building something. c. Debate and discussion.
4. What is your favorite way to relax?	a. Read a book, watch a video, paint. b. Play sports, ride bikes, or walk with friends. c. Talk and hang out with friends, listen to music.
5. When you were in grade school, what was the most likely to get you into trouble?	a. Doodling or writing notes in class, reading a book under the desk. b. Not staying in your seat. c. Talking too much.

Scoring Your Quiz

Count up the numbers of a., b., and c. answers, and write them here.

a. _____ visual

b. _____ physical

c. _____ auditory

Note which one of these has the most answers, and the second most, and the third most.

◎ Draw diagrams, charts, and pictures of the information you are studying.

◎ Break math into logical steps and write them down in those smaller blocks.

◎ Invent visual mnemonics, such as pictures or word games, to help you learn facts. For example, if you have to learn something in science class about the properties of light, you could break the information into seven chunks, and associate each chunk with a color of the rainbow. (Rainbow colors have their own mnemonic: Roy G. Biv—red, orange, yellow, green, blue, indigo, violet). When you get to a question about light, remember a rainbow and from that you can recite the facts.

If You Are a Physical Learner

Go for hands-on learning.
- You should probably sit near the front, which helps AD/HD kids stay focused and less distracted by the other kids in class.
- Take notes to keep your hand moving, but don't worry about spelling, or you will get very frustrated, which doesn't help you learn.
- When you are studying at home, walk around. Keep moving.
- Build models, redo labs, or try to think of some other hands-on way to learn the material, such as drawing pictures and making graphs.
- Put a big dry-erase board or chalkboard on your study area wall, so that you have to stand up to write on it. This keeps you moving, so you are physically involved with studying.
- Sometimes you might get some good out of audio tapes on the subject if you listen to them while you walk around, because then you are moving and studying.
- Twitch (jiggle your foot or tap your pencil) while studying.

If You Are an Auditory Learner

Learning through listening is what most schools emphasize, so you're in luck if you are an auditory learner.
- You might want to tape lectures so you can listen to them as part of your studying.
- Listen to music while you study, if it helps. If it helps, remember which songs you listened to while you studied and you can even ask your teacher if you can listen to music on earphones when you have a test. Then listen to the same music you listened to while you studied. This can help you recall what you were studying.
- When you are trying to memorize things, repeat them out loud or at least hear them in your head.
- Invent goofy word games, rhymes, or raps to help you remember facts.
- You might like study groups where you can talk about the material.
- If you get stuck when you are studying math, try talking your way through it (either out loud or in your head).
- Mutter or whisper to yourself. If you need to do this during tests, ask your teacher if you can sit apart from the others so you don't disturb the other kids (or get laughed at!).
- Ask a friend or family member to quiz you on stuff, so you are telling the answers to someone.

Helen's Sample School Contract

Assignments: Knowing What They Are and Bringing Them Home

◉ Write down my assignment, either in class or at the end of the school day. If I forget an assignment, I will go back to the classroom to check the assignment with the teacher. If I can, I will e-mail myself a copy of the homework assignment from the school computer lab.

◉ I will get the phone number of at least one friend in every class, and call them to check on the assignment if I need to.

◉ If I don't understand the assignment when I actually start doing it, I will call a friend and try to figure it out. If I can't, I will do the best I can with the assignment and try not to get too frustrated, and I will talk to the teacher the next day, either before or after class, or before or after school.

◉ Before I get on the bus to come home, I will try to remember to review my assignment list and get what I need before I get on the bus.

Homework Time and Place

◉ I will do homework in the living room or in my room. I can listen to any kind of music I want, but I cannot turn on the television, since I know that means I will watch television and NOT do homework.

◉ I can use the computer, but I have to limit any game playing or instant messaging or e-mail to ten-minute breaks between doing real homework.

◉ Sometime after I have had an after school snack, Mom will ask me about homework: when, what, how much, and whether she should remind me about it. I won't get mad at her about this.

◉ If I need motivation, I will call a friend, ask Mom to hang out, or set myself some mini-goal on the theory that I can do anything for five minutes. (That is, if I get stuck, I will set a timer and make myself do homework for five minutes to see how far I can get.) Mom promises not to nag or hover unless I want her around or tell her to remind me.

Turning in Homework

◉ When I finish homework, I will immediately put it in my backpack. And if I remember, I'll even put it in a folder. On a really good day I'll put it in the right folder.

◉ If I forget to hand in an assignment, I will talk to the teacher as soon as I remember, or send the teacher an e-mail explaining that I just found the assignment, it was done, and can I turn it in late. This lets the teacher know I am trying to remember.

Payoff

◉ If I get my homework done at night, I can earn a credit towards renting a movie or getting a book. If I get four credits, I get to rent a movie on the weekend. If I get ten credits, I score a trip to the book-store, where I can pick out a book.

The Back Page
• • •

Cheat Sheet

School. Not everybody's favorite. But figuring out your learning style can be very helpful. So can asking for accommodations that are right for you. The main message is keep trying (which you've probably heard a gazillion times). But it's true. And remember that when you find something that you love to do, things will get easier. Just keep on moving. And that's good advice for kids who don't have AD/HD, too!

• • •

Ask Ms. ADDvice Lady

Dear Ms. ADDvice Lady:

Why do I do better in hard classes than I do in do in easy classes? The easier the class is, the worse I do in the class. What does that mean?

Easy F (Not Easy A)

Dear Easy F/A,

For some of us with AD/HD, a challenge is easier than boredom. What that means is that you may want to take hard classes, to keep your attention engaged.

Do you find that sometimes you get the most done when you have the least time? Pressure can be a big help. The trick is to keep yourself from requiring too much pressure. If you let too much pressure pile up, one day you might explode.

So it's helpful to figure out how much pressure you need, except make sure that amount of pressure still leaves enough time to DO the project.

Miss ADDvice Lady

• • •

Fun Facts to Forget

Get some sleep! Research shows that getting a full night's sleep before working out a problem helps you solve the problem. So, if you have something to figure out, a problem to solve, or a math test that you have studied for, go to sleep. In one study, people getting enough sleep were three times as likely to have solved a problem when they woke up than those with an interrupted night's sleep.

• • •

Chapter 12

Friendship and School Stories

We've had a chapter on friends and a chapter on school. Those two things aren't always easy to separate in real life, though. That is, you might have some friends who don't go to your school, but it's pretty hard to make it through school without any friends there. So this chapter talks about both at once.

Bo: My turn. Not that I want one. Not for this story.

When I was in grade school, I had this one friend, Betsy. I didn't want other friends. My mom invited other kids over. I would wonder why. I wanted to play with just Betsy. My mom said I needed more friends. She told me to give Betsy "space."

Fine. I would give her space. And galaxies, too. And stars. Anything she wanted. I wanted to play with just her.

Mom told me it's okay to need one friend. She said that Betsy sometimes might feel smothered, though.

By fifth grade, Betsy hung out with other kids. I got more clingy, according to my mom. I was used to needing one person. But now that she wasn't always there, I was scared and lonely.

Now, when I think about it, Betsy was just okay. I don't know why I stuck to her. And she was bossy, too. I had to do what she wanted me to. But I didn't want to play with anybody else.

During fifth grade, I played with Betsy once in awhile, always at her house. Her mom didn't like me. I was trying to keep Betsy as my best friend. It wasn't working. It was awful.

When I started middle school, Betsy was in only two of my classes. She wouldn't talk to me. It hurt. A lot. I was lonely. I couldn't figure out how to fit in. I was really sad.

My mom made me go to a counselor. After I talked with the counselor a few times, Mom told me I might have AD/HD. Then we went to the doctor. I was worried. I had something that was permanent? I didn't want to have something. I didn't want to be different. And I didn't want to take pills.

But I was so sad and worried that it was easier to take my meds. I didn't want to argue with my mom. After all, she was on my side.

I told you that when I tried AD/HD meds, I got angry real fast. So the doctor put me on anxiety meds. Then life got easier. I found out what it was like not to worry all the time.

Right after that, Mom made me pick two extracurricular activities. I joined a club at school. I even started hanging out with two girls there. So school was better because I had somebody to eat lunch with.

I had to pick another thing to do, too. First I took swimming lessons. I hated them. Then I took dance lessons. I hated them more. Then I took my dog to dog training. I like dog training.

My dog is little but bad. Well, not bad, but badly behaved. She's a mutt. She's mostly black. Her hair is curly, almost like a poodle, and she has the cutest face you ever saw.

Anyway. Dog training classes. I met a girl training her dog. We got to be friends. She is dyslexic, so she knows about special education too. We have stayed good friends.

I'm not friends with Betsy anymore. Now, I am careful around her.

I don't think I'll ever need a lot of friends. Instead, I'll probably need a few close friends.

Helen: My turn. I get along fine with the people on the track team. I also get along fine with a lot of the boys in school. They are so much less complicated than the girls. (I do like this one guy, but that's not the same thing.) I get along okay with a lot of kids.

I was diagnosed in middle school. It wasn't a surprise. I knew I was more active than most girls, and that I talked a lot and was disorganized in a lot of ways.

Actually, I thought it was cool to be diagnosed. I know some kids hate being different, but I already knew I was. So it was a relief.

My mom and I think that I only need a low dose of AD/HD medication partly because of the amount of exercise I get. The exercise I'm always doing mostly takes care of my kind of AD/HD.

Now I'm in a bigger school. I hardly ever see kids from middle school. I like the track team, get along great with a bunch of the guys, and also joined the robotics club. There's a group of girls in the robotics club who are really interesting. The good thing about them is that they are more interested in the projects we work on than in "she-said you-hurt-my-feelings did-you-hear-that"—stuff that I am no good at. So things keep getting better.

Maddy: Me? My turn? I don't have a problem with friends now, but I did for a while during the herding years of middle school. (I call it herding: girls run in bunches, everybody gossips, cliques are everywhere, and everybody else seems to know what to wear and how to put on makeup.) I'll explain more about what I mean in the next section about school personalities.

It Isn't Just You: Schools Have Personalities, Too

Maddy: I've attended four or five schools by now (you've probably been to at least two or three: preschool, elementary school, middle school or junior high, maybe high school), and my current theory is that each school has its own personality. Only one of the schools I've attended so far has Obnoxious Personality Disorder (it isn't a real diagnosis, but it's accurate, at least for this school). To survive school, you need to understand the school's personality, then you need to figure out how to get along, or at least get by, or even better, to do well with that type of school personality.

Let's start from the beginning. You, or whoever you know who has AD/HD, is already impulsive, distractible, fidgety. Now, let's mix that with two common school personalities.

School Personality: Conformist

Maddy: In the dark days of junior high (or middle school, whichever one you are in or used to go to), the girls herd and the key is to fit in…. ooh, sounds like a torture chamber to me. It felt like it, too.

Some schools are full of kids who can follow rules and fit in. The school likes and encourages that. I went to a school like that. The conformist school, I called it. At that school I felt like I had the words LIFELONG LOSER tattooed on my head.

The other kids fit into this rigid school structure somehow, but I couldn't even remember where my locker was, let alone what homework I was supposed to hand in and what I was supposed to be saying and wearing and acting like. Everybody laughed at me because I seemed to lose my shoes a lot, and I wore my sweatshirts inside out when nobody else did, and I had curly hair so nobody could tell if I combed it, and I didn't have a chest or a figure. I cried a lot.

My first mistake, when I started at that school, was that I was friendly and said "hi" to people. This apparently was Not Done, and was Weird. I would introduce myself and the kids would get really quiet and stare at me. The school atmosphere reinforced that attitude, too—it was a big deal to follow the rules and do a lot of homework and fit in. I felt like I was going to school with robots.

A sense of humor alone can make you a total misfit in a place like that.

This is the kind of school that talks about "Your Permanent Record." As if some official document is going to be micro-chipped and inserted under your skin, forever. From that point on, every new person you met would scan you with some instrument, then immediately know everything on your permanent record. For the rest of your life, that person would know you didn't hand in a paper on time, so Mr. Slugingsky gave you a D, and you forgot about the presentation in Ms. Pantelli's class, so everyone laughed at you.

I ended up at the vice principal's office for mouthing off at somebody bossing me, when I didn't know she was a teacher. This was after school. (I hate the word disrespect. I hear how disrespectful I am all the time. I don't think they respect me much, so why should I respect them? That's a whole subject on its own.)

At that point, my mom promised to get me out of that school. We looked at other schools around town, including some private schools. She said it would be okay for me to stay out for a few days, too. Mom pulled me out in December, after I started feeling really stupid and bad.

This is the same school that my older sister did very well in. She likes rules. They give her a kind of camouflage where she can get by doing exactly what's asked, get straight As, and still be very, very free. I envy her ability to do that.

At the new school, I got a 504 plan, and we worked more on getting the right kind of medicine. If we'd done that at the conformist school, I might have gotten by. Not been happy. But gotten by.

But my school district lets you change schools through open enrollment, and so my mom put me in a different school that was another kind of school that I'll talk about in a minute.

Helen: I'm lucky. I can get along. I do go out of my way to get to know my teachers, but that isn't hard for me, since I get along okay with adults, sometimes better than with kids. So I just ask questions and work with the teachers. I also hate getting into trouble like poison. So that motivates me to put energy into getting along.

Bo: My middle school was conformist. I was so anxious that I got obsessive about every-thing. For a little while, I got so compulsive that I pulled out some of my hair. Mom found out and hauled me back to the doctor. The psychiatrist tried a different anxiety medicine. Eventually I felt better and quit the hair pulling.

Maddy: I didn't last at the conformist school. I had no idea what the rules were, written or unwritten. I simply failed and what was worse, I felt like I SHOULD fail because I felt like a LOSER.

School Personality: Nonconformist

Maddy: After I was released from CMS (Conformity Middle School), I went to a different kind of public school that I'll call nonconformist. This school is a lot more relaxed and uses an "experiential" model, which means basically that you get to do more hands-on activities and get out of your seat more. The kids who go there are a lot more open to different kinds of kids. Heck, they even wave and say hi!

I know that not everybody has a choice like I had, and I know I'm lucky. If you don't have a choice and you are having a bad time at your school, remember that there is another life after school, and other kinds of people, too. Even if you have to stick it out, you can read about other kinds of places and that can be a goal—to end up somewhere you can fit in.

I made friends with a lot of kids at the new school. Turns out that school was full of kids like me, who didn't do so well in the neighborhood schools. A lot of the kids had AD/HD, even, along with some other things.

And now I'm in high school, another alternative kind of school that's in the public school system. I'm doing okay. My grades aren't much, but I'm hoping I'll get more organized this year.

Surviving

Maddy: If you are at a school that doesn't match your personality, you have to make an extra effort. Usually schools have some kind of clubs or activities where kids do things you are interested in—band, say, or quiz bowl or a singing group or something. Most schools have kids that don't fit in. The trick is to find kids you like to hang out with, who make you feel okay about your you-ness.

If kids are picking on you or bullying you, tell some trustworthy adult—don't just take it. Do something….And if your school really isn't much of a match, maybe you could find a group in town or at a local university. One kid I know did theater all over town, instead of at her high school, because the high school director didn't like her. Another kid danced in a dance team. Find an ultimate frisbee club, or go online to find other kids interested in the things you are interested in. Be careful with this one, of course—we all know the stories about kids sneaking out to meet people they have met online, then the person turns out to be some predator.

Keep trying. There are other kids like you out there, otherwise there wouldn't be a book like this! Your job is to find those kids. And those kids will be as glad to find you as you are to find them.

The Back Page
• • •

Cheat Sheet

Not every school is alike, and if you are going to a school where you don't seem to fit in, remember that it might, just might, be that the school doesn't fit you very well, as opposed to you being the one who doesn't fit. If that makes sense to you.

Even if you don't fit so well, you can probably find other kids like you—but you might have to find some clubs that you are interested in, or activities—theater, band, skate boarding kids. And don't forget, your town might have other ways to join groups or get involved in things you find interesting, and that might let you find other people with similar interests. Keep trying!

• • •

Ask Ms. ADDvice Lady

Dear Ms. ADDvice Lady:

I always put my foot in my mouth. Always. Every time. We can be talking about something totally benign, like Jello, and I can manage to say the wrong thing. How can I fix this big problem?

Tripping Over My Mouth

Dear Tripping,

I am so sympathetic. I have spent many years trying to extract my foot from my mouth, so I feel well qualified to speak on this issue.

Several habits can help, although I can be counted on, when too tired, very tense, or self-conscious and nervous, to say the wrong thing, typically in a fairly spectacular way. What does work is to practice listening, to say as little as possible, and to echo back what you hear the other person saying. These strategies simply work, and work well.

Easy to say, hard to do.

If I know something is coming up that will likely be stressful (college interview, party with someone I would like to impress or become friends with, etc.), I remind myself all day, every time I think about the upcoming situation, to *say very little, echo back, and listen hard.* I write it down, say it to myself, over and over. This works pretty well. Once I start to relax, I can enter the swing of the conversation less self-consciously or more calmly.

The problem is that sometimes the situation arises without time to prepare. When I suddenly find myself in such a situation without warning, I try to pause, that same pause I'm always inserting anyway before I act impulsively. During that pause I try to remind myself of the big three (be quiet, echo, listen).

Lastly, when I do stick my foot in it, I try not to beat myself up. After all, everyone makes mistakes. The trick (especially tricky for someone with AD/HD) is to try to remember what you learned and to apply it the next time your foot is inching toward your mouth.

•••

Fun Facts to Forget

For fifty years, researchers thought that when humans got stressed, a cascade of brain chemicals led to a "fight or flight" reaction. (They were partly right, too.) If you are being chased by a saber-tooth tiger, this is a logical set of choices. This conclusion is the result of decades of researchers (mostly men) studying men's reactions to stress.

In 2000, some (women) researchers looked at women's reaction to stress. The same fight or flight release of brain chemicals happens in women, but additional chemicals are also released in the female brain. Part of this extra cascade of brain chemicals includes the release of the hormone oxtyocin. This hormone buffers the fight or flight reaction, and encourages women to "tend and befriend." On top of that, the more tending and befriending, the more the oxytocin, and the calmer the stress reaction.

•••

Chapter 13

The Lightbulb Has to Want to Change

And the day came when the risk to remain tight in a bud was more painful than the risk it took to blossom.

—sometimes attributed to Anais Nin.

This is the hardest part of AD/HD. The part that means that it's up to YOU.

The only way to deal with AD/HD is to decide to deal with it, then deal with it. And that decision, along with the effort, is yours. Nobody can do it for you.

It's hard work to change, but you can do it. And it's worth it. Get the help you need from parents, books like this, counselors, medicines if they work for you, and friends and teachers, but it's your job to deal with the AD/HD.

You can do it!

You pretty much get as much out of any of these treatments as you want. (See the light bulb joke, next page.) It is hard work to try all these things, though.

So if you are *not* ready to change, save your parents and yourself time, frustration, and money, and wait until you are up to it. Part of this is doing it when YOU are ready to.

You have to have confidence in your ability, and then be tough enough to follow through. — Rosalynn Carter

The Back Page
• • •

Cheat Sheet

Question: How many psychiatrists does it take to change a light bulb?
Answer: Just one, but the light bulb has to want to change.

• • •

Fun Facts to Forget

Self-control gets harder as the day goes along. Essentially, you can use it up, and sleep helps you refresh your stash of self-control. Researchers examined whether willpower was a thought process, a skill that could be learned, or essentially something that consumed energy.

The scientists' research showed that self-control consumes energy. Hard to argue with that one.

• • •

Chapter 14

More Survival Tactics

Since I have AD/HD, you could guess that maybe I don't have the best organizational skills in the world. I tried to divide everything in this book into neat little chapters, but some survival tips were left over when I got to the end of the book. Here they are.

Some General AD/HD Survival Tips

So, here are some most excellent things that have helped in the past, depending on the day:

The Tool	How You Might Make It Work For You
Make it a game or a race.	Sometimes I like to see how fast I can do something. That way it feels less like a chore or whatever. So, I'll see how fast I can fold the clothes in the dryer, stuff like that.
Solve the problem in an unusual or creative way.	Once I realize something is a problem, I like to think up new ways to solve it that are at least not boring. For example, to memorize stuff I can sing it—make up a melody or use some tune I know. Or if I am organizing my locker at school, I bring in boxes covered with contact paper and different kinds of bags decorated whatever way. I can stick pencils and pens into the small boxes, books that have to go home in another. You get the idea. Best of all, it's organized but not dull.

Lists, writing down things you need to remember.

Write stuff down and put it someplace you'll see it. I have pockets on everything. Also, if I put stuff in my shoes, then I know where it is. Of course, the list might be smelly.... also, money gets smelly there too, so now I put that in my sock. As you can see, though, it's on my person somewhere.

My backpack has become a safe place to put stuff. All those zipper pockets keep things inside the backpack, so at least I don't lose them. Also, my bus pass is tied to my backpack with packing tape. I don't lose that anymore, either.

I also e-mail myself reminders, and do my homework on the computer and e-mail the homework to myself so I can print it out at school, especially if I printed out the homework, then left it at home.

One problem with making lists is remembering: 1) where they are and 2) that they exist. So put the list somewhere that you will see it, the more weird or irritating, the better. You might put it on your doorknob, or on the mirror, or wherever you know you are going to look, and when you see the list, right away do the stuff on it. This helps you get extra stuff done before you go to bed. And if you're like me and you hate going to bed anyway, then that's a good time. Just make sure that what's on the list isn't "READ A 600 PAGE BOOK BEFORE MORNING."

Buddy system.

I call up a friend and we talk while I do the dishes. It's the best way to get through that tedium. Also, good for homework, if you have a friend in the same class. You can talk about the problems while you do them. The only trick for me is that I need to do the homework, not have so much fun with my friend that the assignment doesn't get done.

If this, then that.

If I have something I don't want to do, then I promise myself something after. For example, I don't get to spend much time with my friends who don't go to my school. So instead I promise myself that I get to call them the instant I am done with my homework.

The piling principle.

This is my main way of organizing. At school, one teacher lets me leave stuff in her room. At home, I pile up what I need for school before I go to bed. My backpack is basically a mobile pile, with everything I can think I might need for the day or the outing or in general.

20-second rule.

If you are especially worried that you might forget something and it is important, either write it down within the next 20 seconds, tell someone within the 20 seconds to remind you, or repeat it over and over and over while you hunt for a pen and paper or a friend who will help you remember it.

Sheets shield the mess.

Sometimes, to shut out distractions, I'll drape blankets over everything in my messy room except what I'm working on. I might still get distracted, but less than if all the clutter is always visible.

Tie it to something else you do anyway.	This is related to the "brush your teeth before you go to bed" rule. So hook together something you need to remember to something you already do. That helps make it a habit.
	Now, before I go to bed, I shower, pile stuff on my backpack, and find my shoes. And I keep my meds in the bathroom, because I always end up there at some point in the morning. Right when I see them, I take them.
	See. These are all hooked to something I do everyday, anyway.

Humor

I don't think I need to say anything else about this one, except that keeping your sense of humor may help you keep your sanity. A lot of times, if I forget things, I can make a joke and that way people laugh with me, not at me. "I know you aren't going to believe this, since I am so organized at all times, but I forgot to bring…."

Helen: Please, can I laugh at you?

Maddy: You can, Helen, but only you.

Keep Trying!

Winston Churchill (another famous guy who likely had AD/HD) said:
"Never, ever, ever, ever, give up."
I like that.

What to Change and How Much at Once

I try to change the stuff about AD/HD that I really hate, like losing homework and making people feel like I'm not listening to them. It's hard to sort out which parts to change and which to leave alone, but you still have to try lots of combinations until you find something that works for you and that feels more right than wrong.

When you decide to work on things to make your life easier, don't, DO NOT, try to fix everything at once. Pick one thing or only a few things. Then work on that one thing. For example, maybe your goal is to get up in the mornings without so much trouble. Think about ways to accomplish that every night and every morning. Maybe go to bed earlier. Or put boring books by your bed so you'll fall asleep. Me? I put hard-to-read nonfiction books by my bed, like about geology. I pick one up and go right to sleep. And when I wake up, I sometimes make myself stand up right away, even if my eyes are still closed, and start stumbling around the room. Then I am awake in spite of myself.

Or, say you want to work on keeping your room more organized. Spend five minutes on that every day, before doing something you want to do—like watching TV or calling a friend up on the phone. Or find a friend who also wants to clean up her room and you can clean up your rooms while you talk on the phone.

Keep it do-able.

> Comparison is the seat of all unhappiness.
> —The Buddha

The Perfect Girl

Watch out about this one: don't compare yourself to The Perfect Girl. She's always in your life. She does everything right—she might be you in some alternate universe. If you *do* find you are always watching some girl like that, try to get to know her. Every time I've done that, I've discovered that the person is human and that she has troubles and isn't perfect. That makes me feel better.

Also, about the perfect girl: Instead of concentrating on all that she does well, concentrate on what you do well—remind yourself of the good things about yourself.

In fact, while you're at it, don't compare yourself to anyone.

Cut yourself some slack. Do what you can do. You're not going to be like everybody else. You can still be really successful, just in your own way.

You Don't Have to Do It Alone

This is a lot to have to deal with.

But one thing is for sure. You don't have to do it alone. I really liked finding out that it wasn't just me, that I wasn't lazy or useless or hopeless.

Even if you can't see a counselor or get a coach, or if you don't want to, you can still get some help. A lot of us girls with AD/HD are out here, and we can help each other. You might ask a teacher or coach or whoever if they know any other girls with AD/HD that you could talk to. Another great way to get support is through more reading about AD/HD and checking out some AD/HD organizations and their web sites.

You can also search the web for information about AD/HD. But be careful or you could end up at sites talking about herbal treatments or that Ritalin Is Evil or AD/HD isn't real, it's a way to control our children, or whatever. Which you can read, because it doesn't hurt to know how some (uninformed) people feel about AD/HD, but I think it's discouraging.

National AD/HD organizations (and their local chapters, which means people in your town or area who are members of the national organization and get together nearby) can be helpful too. The organizations can send you information, if you don't have easy access to the Internet. Online you could maybe find a bulletin board or chat room where you can ask questions. You may also be able to attend conventions or meetings and meet other people with AD/HD.

Some groups, books, and other things that can help are listed on the next two pages.

ADDitude magazine
P.O. Box 500
Missouri City, TX 77459
646-366-0830; 646-366-0842 (fax)
www.additudemag.com
    You can find this at bookstores or maybe your library. (If your library doesn't carry it, you can ask a librarian to please consider carrying it!)

ADDA (Attention Deficit Disorder Association)
P.O. Box 543
Pottstown, PA 19464
484-945-2101; 610-970-7520 (fax)
www.add.org

CHADD (CHildren and Adults with Attention Deficit hyperactivity Disorder)
8181 Professional Place, Suite 150,
Landover, MD 20785
800-233-4050; 301-306-7090 (fax)
www.chadd.org

Gantos, Jack. *Joey Pigza Loses Control.* New York: Farrar Straus and Giroux, 2000.

Hallowell, Edward M. and John Ratey. *Driven to Distraction: Recognizing and Coping with Attention Deficit Disorder from Childhood to Adulthood.* New York: Simon & Schuster, 1994

LDOnline
www.ldonline.org

National Center for Gender Issues & AD/HD
2775 South Quincy Street,
Arlington, VA 22206
888-238-8588; 207-244-9933 (fax)
www.ncgiadd.org

Novotni, Michele. *What Does Everybody Else Know That I Don't? Social Skills Help for Adults with Attention Deficit/Hyperactivity Disorder.* Plantation, FL: Specialty Press, 1999.

    Some other books on the subject that you might want to read, but that were written for parents and teachers:

Dendy, Chris A. Ziegler. *Teenagers with ADD: A Parents' Guide.* Bethesda, MD: Woodbine House, 1995.

Dendy, Chris A. Ziegler. *Teaching Teens with ADD and ADHD*. Bethesda, MD: Woodbine House, 2000.

Horacek, H. Joseph. *Brainstorms: Understanding and Treating the Emotional Storms of Attention Deficit Hyperactivity Disorder from Childhood through Adulthood*. Northvale, NJ: Jason Aronson, 1998.

Manassis, Katharina and Anne Marie Levac. *Helping Your Teenager Beat Depression*. Bethesda, MD: Woodbine House, 2004.

Nadeau, Kathleen G., Ellen Littman, and Patricia O. Quinn. *Understanding Girls with AD/HD*. Silver Spring, MD: Advantage Books, 2000.

Strauch, Barbara. *The Primal Teen: What the New Discoveries about the Teenage Brain Tell Us about Our Kids*. New York, NY: Doubleday, 2003.

There's a lot more out there too. If you don't find what you need, maybe you can start your own organization!

The Back Page
●●●

Cheat Sheet

You can do something about AD/HD to help you deal with the chaos that can go along with it. And you don't have to do it alone—get help! It's out there, because other girls with AD/HD are out there, too. Check out a few books or web sites or magazines, stay informed!

●●●

Ask Ms. ADDvice Lady

Dear Ms. ADDvice Lady:

My aunt knows that I have been diagnosed with AD/HD, but she says that I can focus when I want to, and asks me why my grades are so bad. This started when she visited over winter break, and everybody in the family, including my aunt and me, worked on a puzzle we had set up. She knows I did pretty much the entire 1000-piece puzzle. Even so, I can't make myself concentrate on homework, so my grades aren't very good.

Is she right? What do I say to her?

Puzzled AD/HDer

Dear Puzzled,

Your aunt is uninformed. I suggest you give her this book or some other book on AD/HD on her birthday or the next gift-giving occasion. In my experience, sometimes it's hard for people to understand things that they haven't experienced themselves. Apparently your AD/HD symptoms are something she doesn't know much about, so she's attributing the behavior to an absence of trying.

How trying for you.

Your aunt is NOT correct when she says you can focus when you want to. You can focus when your attention fastens onto something. That's not the same as focusing on things that do not snatch your attention.

The best favor anyone can do for the rest of the people with AD/HD in the world is help those, like your aunt, who are uninformed become informed. You aunt will then not only understand you, but thousands of other people like you, undoubtedly including many people she works with, has gone to school with, or otherwise meets throughout her life.

I suggest a book simply because a book is objective. Your aunt may not be able to imagine anyone who cannot focus when they want to, so conversation may not be sufficient.

Good luck!

Miss ADDvice Lady

...

Fun Facts to Forget

The first time-organizer/planner is attributed to a lawyer, Morris Perkins, who developed one in 1947 to manage his time. He called this organizer "Lawyer's Day." From this came an onslaught of planners of all types, including homework planners.

Now we know who to thank (or blame) for planners!

...

Afterword

Hurrah and congratulations. You are now at the end of the book, and you know more about AD/HD than when you started. (At least, I hope you do!)

If you have gone to the trouble of reading any of this book, then you are doing a good job. Sure, there are some hard parts to having AD/HD, but most of the time I would rather be who I am with the AD/HD. I like who I am. I am spontaneous. I have a sense of humor. And energy. And focus for the things I like to do.

I spoke with a famous doctor who has AD/HD, has written a ton of books on AD/HD, and is running a center for girls and women with AD/HD. I asked her—her name is Dr. Patricia Quinn—what she would say to girls like me with AD/HD. She looked at me, paused, and said, "I would tell them that everything is going to be okay." I like that. I think everything will be okay, too, and I think having AD/HD can be a good thing, something unique, and part of me.

So, let's go make some history!

Selected Bibliography

For a more complete bibliography, visit www.bethwalker.com

"Anxiety Disorders." NIH Publication No. 97-3879, Printed 1994, Reprinted 1995, 1997. Http://mentalhealth.about.com/cs/anxietypanic/l/blanxiety.htm

Barkley, Russell A. *Taking Charge of ADHD.* New York: Guildford Press, 2000.

Bower, Bruce. "Attention Loss: ADHD May Lower Brain Volume." *Science News,* Oct.12, 2002.

Cowan, Nelson. "The Magical Number 4 in Short Term Memory: A Reconsideration of Mental Storage Capacity." *Behavioral and Brain Sciences,* 24 (1), 2001.

Crawford, Nicole. "ADHD: A Women's Issue: Psychologists Are Fighting Gender Bias Research in Attention-Deficit Hyperactivity Disorder." *Monitor on Psychology,* 34 (2), Feb. 2003, page 28. also: http://www.apa.org/monitor/feb03/adhd.html

Dendy, Chris Ziegler. *Teenagers with ADD: A Parents' Guide.* Bethesda, MD: Woodbine House, 1995.

Diagnostic and Statistical Manual of Mental Disorders, Fourth Edition. Washington, D.C.: American Psychiatric Association, 1994.

Hallowell, Edward M. and John Ratey. *Driven to Distraction.* New York: Simon & Schuster, 1994.

Hinshaw, Stephen. "Preadolescent Girls with Attention-Deficit/Hyperactivity Disorder." *Journal of Consulting and Clinical Psychology,* 70 (5).

Horacek, H. Joseph. *Brainstorms: Understanding and Treating the Emotional Storms of Attention Deficit Hyperactivity Disorder from Childhood through Adulthood.* Northvale, NJ: Jason Aronson, 1998.

Nadeau, Kathleen G., Ellen Littman, and Patricia O. Quinn. *Understanding Girls with AD/HD.* Silver Spring, MD: Advantage Books, 2000.

Novotni, Michele. *What Does Everybody Else Know That I Don't?* Plantation, FL: Specialty Press, 1999.

Reiff, Michael I., ed. *ADHD: A Complete and Authoritative Guide.* Elk Grove Village, IL: The American Academy of Pediatrics, 2004.

Strauch, Barbara. *The Primal Teen: What the New Discoveries about the Teenage Brain Tell Us about Our Kids.* New York: Doubleday, 2003.

Index